Praise for *Dumped*

"This remarkable collection provides an exhilarating range of voices exploring what happens when female friendships falter. Wise, compassionate, and smart, each of these essays is a revelation. Give your best friend a copy along with a warm, thankful hug."

—**Dinty W. Moore**, author, *The Mindful Writer*

"*Dumped* touches a nerve from page one. It touches on a subject that all women know too well, yet is complicated and painful to articulate: the mourning, and sometimes redemption, that comes from being dumped by a sister-like friend. For every woman who has ever drowned her sorrows in a pint of ice cream over the loss of a close friend—or simply needs to know she is not alone—this book is for her."

—**Elisa Batista**, publisher of MotherTalkers.com,
a Daily Kos community

"This very honest, very human, and often very hilarious book made me laugh, cry, nod, squirm, and think anew about friendships gone by. Big applause to Nina Gaby, and all the contributors, for crystallizing so finely the inescapable life experience that is the end of a friendship."

—**Suzanne Strempek Shea**, author of
*This Is Paradise: An Irish Mother's Grief,
an African Village's Plight, and the Medical
Clinic That Brought Fresh Hope to Both*

"The essays in *Dumped* are ferocious and loving, devastating and hopeful, insightful and perplexing. A savage, thorny look at friendship . . . and a rare, uncensored, sometimes terrifying glimpse into the female psyche."

—**Neil White**, author of
In the Sanctuary of Outcasts and publisher

"What goes on between men and women has been examined in literature for many years. This terrific collection of stories, however, probes the largely unexplored, perhaps sacrosanct, territory of what goes on between women. Lively and astute, candid and wrenching, the pieces reveal the clumsy dismantling not just of friendships but also of our own notions of ourselves as friends, meaning our own capacities—sometimes limited, sometimes capacious—for relationships with other women. An enlightening and long-overdue collection."

—**Barbara Hurd**, author of *Walking the Wrack Line*

"In these essays lie honest portraits of break-ups of the most ancient kind, blood letting stone, an abrupt jolt that equals part orphan, part refugee. We leave our sisters suddenly, without warning or explanation, beside the road of untamed life. Rudderless, without us. Without each other. And therein lies the key, I knew the moment Nina mentioned this collection that she was on to something. A hotspot of not only what ignites us breaks our hearts as well."

—**River Jordan**, author of *Praying for Strangers*

"*Dumped* is an often revelatory, heart-wrenching compendium, immensely readable, fascinating in its tragic familiarity, and among the best books available on the tenacity of our human desire to connect, and stay connected, even with those with whom the connections were, in the final analysis, ephemeral and fleeting."

—**Burl Barer**, author of *Man Overboard* and *Body Count*

dumped

dumped

STORIES OF
WOMEN
UNFRIENDING
WOMEN

Edited by Nina Gaby

SHE WRITES PRESS

Published 2015
Printed in the United States of America
ISBN: 978-1-63152-954-2
Library of Congress Control Number: 2014956082

For information, address:
She Writes Press
1563 Solano Ave #546
Berkeley, CA 94707

She Writes Press is a division of Spark Point Studio, LLC.

"How I Lost Her," by Ann Hood, was previously published in Jenny Offill and Elissa Schappell, eds., The Friend Who Got Away: Twenty Women's True-Life Tales of Friendships that Blew Up, Burned Out, or Faded Away (New York: Broadway Books, 2005). Reprinted with the author's permission.

A slightly different version of "Ten Days," by Suzanne Herman, was previously published in Heather Tosteson and Charles D. Brockett, eds., Connected: What Remains As We All Change (Atlanta: Wising Up Press, 2013). Reprinted with the author's permission.

The contributors have changed some names, places, and recognizable details to protect the privacy of friends and family members mentioned in some of these essays.

Excerpt from "Autotomy" from POEMS NEW AND COLLECTED 1957-1997 by Wislawa Szymborksa, translated from the Polish by Stanislaw Baranczak and Clare Cavanagh. English translation copyright (c) 1998 by Houghton Mifflin Harcourt Publishing Company. Reprinted by permission of Houghton Mifflin Harcourt Publishing Company. All rights reserved.

To my husband, Craig Smith,
who still hasn't dumped me.

And my mother, Ruth Gaby, who always
thought I should have known better.

In danger, the holothurian cuts itself in two.
It abandons one self to the hungry world
and with the other self it flees.

It violently divides into doom and salvation,
retribution and reward, what has been and what will be.

An abyss appears in the middle of its body
between what instantly becomes two foreign shores.

From *Autonomy, Poems New and Collected*
Wislawa Szymborska

"Bitches be bitches"

Ladies' room stall, mall, Western New York

Contents

Part One: When the Herd Turns

Groups are easily swayed by conflict. For some,
the desertion must have felt like a stampede.

Part Two: It's Not Always About You

Against the impossible. Author as bystander,
holding the unfortunate mirror.

Part Three: Blurred Lines

Friendship viewed through a murky lens.
What did we really want to see?

Part Four: Women Remember

Striving for balance.

Part Five: Making Sense of It

Finding meaning in the negative spaces.

Foreword

Victoria Zackheim

Aristotle defined friendship as a "single soul dwelling in two bodies."[1] In Nina Gaby's *Dumped: Stories of Women Unfriending Women*, twenty-five post-Aristotelian writers explore the painful experience of *unfriending*, a word recently conferred a rather prominent place in our social media-driven lexicon. To fully comprehend the trauma of a friend severing ties with us—or, as Gaby words it, of being unfriended and unceremoniously dumped—we must first understand the importance of friendship.

The friendship between women—whether we harken back to the biblical, historical, literary, or junior high school variety—has ever been an alliance in which we share parts of our selves: secrets, fears, petty gossip. We enter into this relationship with the belief that what we confide will remain private, protected.

We trust friendship, put our faith in it, sometimes forget how precious it is, and occasionally betray it. When it works, when the connection is true and safe and heartfelt, it is magic: a hand that calms, a smile that encourages, a voice that soothes, a text or e-mail that urges us to inhale . . . and then to exhale. In whatever form, friendship is a presence reminding us that we are never alone.

When a friendship that has sustained us suddenly disappears, we are left emotionally and physically raw . . . bereft. All the women in this collection have addressed heart-on the meaning of friendship in its many forms, and the consequences of a friendship gone bad.

Anaïs Nin wrote that "each friend represents a world in us, a world possibly not born until they arrive, and it is only by this meeting that a new world is born."[2] If, as she says, every friend who comes into our lives introduces us to a new (and wonder-filled) way to live in the world, a new way to *be*, then finding ourselves suddenly without that connection leaves us staring into a chasm so deep as to appear without end. Perhaps reading these very personal stories will be a reminder to all of us that friendship is very often what centers our lives.

Victoria Zackheim is the author of the novel, The Bone Weaver, *and editor of six anthologies, the latest being* Faith: Essays from Believers, Agnostics, and Atheists *(Beyond Words/Atria/Simon & Schuster, 2015). Victoria adapted essays from her first anthology,* The Other Woman, *and created a play now in development. Another play,* Entangled, *is in development with Z Space Theater, San Francisco. Victoria wrote the screenplay* Maidstone, *a feature film in development, and the documentary film* Where Birds Never Sang: The Story of Ravensbrück and Sachsenhausen Concentration Camps, *which aired nationwide on PBS. She created Women's Voices, a multi-author program now being presented in the United States and scheduled in the UK in 2015. She teaches "Personal Essay" in the UCLA Extension Writers' Program, and is a frequent speaker and instructor at writing conferences and for women's organizations in the U.S., Mexico, Canada, the UK and France.*

Introduction

You picked up this book. If the title resonates for you or for someone you care about, maybe you are one of the more than 160 million women in America today for whom friendships are vitally important. It is this primacy that makes the pain of being dumped by a woman friend so excruciating. We feel abandoned, discarded . . . betrayed. We expect the occasional workplace disasters, and we learn to survive the end of romantic relationships; after all, we have our chums to prop us up when bad things happen. But when a woman—someone with whom we've shared thoughts, feelings, fears—ends a friendship, how do we cope? In this collection, these gifted writers explore that near-universal experience of being unfriended by those from whom we expected more.

It is a somewhat new and very welcome development that the stories of our friendships have become more marketable and even more scientifically relevant. According to the *Los Angeles Times*, 4.6 million viewers watched the season two finale of *Girls* on HBO, and the *Hollywood Reporter* announced an equal number in season three. The successes of *Sex and the City, Mean Girls, Bridesmaids,* and *Orange is the New Black* have been huge. Books about us are making best-seller lists. This is "The Age of Girlfriends," as Anna Holmes, founder of the website Jezebel, wrote in her *New Yorker* essay of the same name. Suddenly we are no longer trivial; we are hot.

So how does all that play out for us normal women? Is there now a pressure in how we view ourselves and our friendships? It turns out that these relationships are good for our physical and mental health too, and that doesn't make these breakups any easier. Associate Chair of Psychiatry and Behavioral Sciences at Stanford University School of Medicine, Professor David Spiegel, said in a March 2010 presentation, "One of the best things that a man could do for his health is to be married to a woman, whereas for a woman one of the best things she could do for her health was to nurture her relationships with her girlfriends." [3]

Spiegel found that women survivors of breast cancer fared better, almost twofold, when they were in social relationships with other women. Our friendships with other women are powerful stuff. Long seen as a buffer against negative experience, the research now suggests that these friendships have the potential to decrease chronically elevated stress hormones such as cortisol, and to increase feel-good and protective neurochemicals such as serotonin, dopamine, and oxytocin. There is an exquisite process in which the midbrain can be protected from damage with enough psychosocial supports, reducing depression and improving quality and quantity of life—an amazing thing. Unless we're talking about breakups. In which case we must wonder: Are we risking our very mortality when we screw up our friendships?

What happens when these support mechanisms are taken away? The twenty-five essays in *Dumped* aren't stories of friendship dying a mutually agreed-upon death, or about falling out of touch and a decade later finding you haven't missed a beat. These are stories written by both established and emerging writers who, like you, may have found themselves erased, without context, possibly without worth. These kinds of experiences leave you angry, confused, even at times feeling undefined. The stories these women tell are ones that will stay with you, maybe for a lifetime. *Dumped*, like a good friend, listens, explores, explains. Some of these are stories for a thicker skin; others are stories that speak to larger issues: issues of resilience, alienation, and repair. Community and context. Stories that redefine us.

My own experiences with being dumped—oh yes, many times—provide the inspiration for this book. In my essay, "Simple Geometry: The Art of War for Girls," I reflect on the loss of my first best-friendship, that earliest of extra-familial bonds: the relationship that first sharpened the lines of definition in the picture of the individual I was about to become. Grieving subsequent losses, often with the ensuing depression and isolation hinted at in the research, I experienced a stark landscape that still confuses me, leaving me to ask these too-universal questions: *Why didn't I see this coming? Is something wrong with me? What do I do now?* In my case, repair did not happen in any traditional manner, no final scene of reconciliation. Instead I found an acceptance, and eventually, as I continue to process it even now, a recognition that I am proud to have lived my life with an ability to care deeply and take risks.

As a psychotherapist for the past quarter century, I know these are the fundamental fears for most of us when confronted with rejection: *Is something wrong with me? Do I deserve this?* It is only through unflinching honesty and self-appraisal that we are able to ask the hard questions and eventually to find solace and meaning.

Each essay in this collection reflects a similar honesty. The ability of these writers to reflect their deepest fears about themselves is what makes their narratives so powerful. This honesty, this lack of distortion, can make the answer to the question *Why did this happen to me?* that much harder to bear. But also that much more compelling to read.

Sometimes it really has nothing to do with you. Sometimes the shadow self of your friend as she attempts to avoid her own reality is the real problem—the very fact that you know her so well is the death blow. In Carol Cassara's *Keeping Secrets*, intimacy becomes intolerable through no fault of the narrator. In *All Talk and Trousers*, Carrie Kabak is admittedly no match for the lilting bullshit brogue of her philandering boyfriend—but what about her deceptive girlfriend?

Some of the stories are about early desertion; indeed, it is almost as if several of our writers attended the same high school. For them, early adolescence became a battlefield where each one confronted the same sense of helplessness, each taking a different course of action. For others, such as Jessica Handler and Ann Hood, surviving unthinkable losses speaks to holding on even tighter, questioning what it would be like to lose the remaining thread of collective memory.

As we explore what really pulls us together or forces us apart, we often find a murky interface in what appears to us as friendship; we try to understand what we are really searching for. Kristabelle Munson, Penny Guisinger, and Jennifer Lang brilliantly show us what it means to seek affiliation and instead to find the alchemy of blurred boundaries.

When she was ten years old, Alexis Paige thought she had learned everything she needed to know about the nature of women from reading *Cosmo* on the beach. Other writers come by their insight unwillingly—as Elayne Clift describes in her thoughtful *Literary Lessons and a Circle of Crones*—through the lens of a fraying support system. And for some, there is no insight to be found: simple acceptance becomes its own reward.

As we explore the fragile and unfathomable nature of lost friendship, we find our own resilience in the stories of others, these wise memes, these templates for redefinition. Lost friendships, betrayal, emptiness, lessons learned—the unthinkable leaves us in that dark place, but only for a while. We rebound because we must, because we are vital. And we rebound because loss, among other things, only serves to make us stronger and to make what remains that much more precious.

Nina Gaby

Part One:
When the Herd Turns

*Groups are easily swayed by conflict. For some, the desertion
must have felt like a stampede.*

The Hate Note

Lindsey Kemp

She told me I had ranch dressing on my chin. I always had something on my chin, or in my teeth, or on my nose, or in my hair. One time, I had bread crumbs sprinkled over one of my eyebrows.

"And you have a piece of chicken stuck right here," Emma said as she pointed to her own front tooth.

I had eaten a truckload of chicken that day. That's the kind of thing I remember about April 9, 2007—the chipotle chicken panini, grilled chicken salad, and cream of chicken soup that I shoveled into my mouth during Emma's thirty-minute lunch break. I don't recall what either of us wore, or where in the South Jersey deli we sat, but I remember the velvety texture of the soup, the moistness of the farm-raised chicken, the ease of our conversation, and the way I wore my lunch on my face like a toddler.

I wiped my chin and used the straw from my iced coffee to dig out the food from my teeth. I looked down at my cell phone, which sat next to Emma's tray of salad and more salad. We had fifteen minutes left before Emma had to return to work, and as usual, I was famished from having to sustain all five-foot-four, 165 pounds of me. Like a wolf ready to attack a coop of clucking poultry, I bared my teeth and tore into my sandwich.

"I still hate my job," Emma said. She shoved a hunk of lettuce into her mouth and played with her side-swept, coffee-colored bangs as she chewed. "I do too much sitting. Why do sales assistants sit so much?"

I assured her that I too hated my job, that working nights made me feel like a zombie, and that I could never pass the standardized tests I scored. I dipped my panini into my cup of soup.

"Chicken on chicken," Emma said. "Nice." She stabbed her salad with her fork. "So have you talked to Adam-poo lately?"

Adam and I had dated during my junior and senior years of college, but we'd had trust issues and broken up after graduation.

"Yeah, last week. We had another fight. He thinks that when I say 'I still care about you' I really mean, 'Can we please be boyfriend and girlfriend again?'"

Emma rolled her eyes. Her perfectly sculpted eyebrows rose up into her bangs. "Good God. Adam, what are you thinking? It's only been eight months," she said.

"I mean maybe one day, if he can learn what the word *honesty* means," I said. I checked my phone for the time. We had five minutes left, and I still had half a sandwich to eat. "I'll e-mail you the details. But spoiler alert: we slept together anyway."

"Oh honey, nooooo," Emma said. She lifted her plastic knife and pretended to impale her heart.

"You know gingers are my weakness. Anyway, what about you? Any sexy time with Scott?"

"Scott's so damn hot, but no. He's too busy banging some girl from his grad class," Emma said. I gasped.

"He's still telling you about *other* girls? Stop putting up with this shit!"

Emma smiled. "In other exciting news," she said, "I just discovered that my roommate's addicted to stealing silverware and coffee mugs from diners."

"And why does she do this?"

"For the thrill, I suppose. This morning I caught her in the kitchen, staring into an open drawer of stolen treasures, admiring her loot." I laughed and threw a used creamer cup at her. She ducked. "I'm harboring a criminal. A-no-ther strike for purg-a-tor-y," Emma sang. (She had been concerned—yet amused—about purgatory ever since eighth grade, when our CCD teacher, Mr. Jones, told us that's where our sinning souls suffered punishment, for eternity! Emma enjoyed documenting our rebellious behavior by adding strikes to a mental scoreboard, which may have been a sin itself.)

"I made out with a guy I met at a bar the other night," I said.

Emma squeaked like a rubber squeeze toy and added a thousand strikes to my score.

"His name is Timmy Wordell. I met him at Kildare's. He has an accent like Rocky Balboa," I said, my mouth full. "And he calls himself T-Word."

"Sounds like a winner," Emma said. The scent of fresh lemon rose from her tea. She sipped it and smiled. Long-lined dimples framed her mouth like parentheses. A few summers before, when she'd been twenty pounds heavier, she'd had bigger cheeks and a rosier glow. I was glad she was healthier, but sometimes I missed the softer Emma. "Speaking of T-Word, you eat like a T. Rex. You know this, right?" she asked.

"Roar," I said. A piece of chicken fell out of my sandwich and onto the table. Emma flicked it at me and pretended to gag when it landed on my chest.

"This is my favorite part, but by my favorite part I mean least favorite, as in 'I want to die,'" I said. Emma leaned in closer. I pulled the lid off my iced coffee and used a spoon to fish for a piece of ice.

"*Lindsey,*" she said. She had no patience.

"He looks like Flea from the Red Hot Chili Peppers."

"Oh, *sexy.*"

"Is it, though? Is it *really?*"

We finished eating, walked to the parking lot, and hugged, but when I got to my car I realized that I had forgotten to ask her about Hanson.

Emma's Hanson obsession began in 1996, when the band released its first (to many, their only) hit, "MMMbop." She traveled the country to see them play live and eventually befriended the band members.

Emma had recently returned from a Hanson concert in California, which was *the one thing* I was supposed to ask about, the thing which had been our reason for "doing lunch." Years later this moment would haunt me.

I ran to her car and motioned for her to roll down the window.

"I'm such an idiot," I said. "How was California?"

Emma checked her car clock.

"I'm going to be late," she said.

"But I want to know," I said. "I'm a moron, I'm sorry, I completely forgot to ask."

Emma laughed and shook her head. "Next time," she said, and then drove away.

When I got back to work, Emma sent me a MySpace message:

i forget if i said thankssss!!!! for coming all the way out here for lunch, but if i didn't, then kissy kissy thank you thank you. if i did, then forget the thank you, just kisses. have fun at work... however difficult it may be.

I responded immediately and asked again about Hanson, but it didn't matter. Emma never answered.

In seventh grade, my best friend from elementary school, Marcy, and her new best friend from our middle school, Crystal, wrote the Hate Note. The Hate Note, written on a piece of notebook paper, contained the following heartwarming message:

> Lindsey,
> I hate you. I was just pretending to be your friend. Crystal hates you, too. You are really annoying. No one likes you. Here's a list of all the people who don't like you:

Fifty kids signed the note. They were kids I had known since I was five, kids I had just met in middle school, and kids I didn't know knew me.

> P.S. Have a great day! Hahahaha!
> Love,
> Marcy and Crystal

They had a boy from my neighborhood hand me the note during my walk home from school. He laughed as he watched me read it three or four times.

No one liked me? *No one?*

The sounds of the street—passing cars, lawn mowers, birds singing—became muted, as if I were wearing earmuffs. My eyes blurred with tears, but I blinked them away.

I ran home and showed my mom the note. When Caitlin, my twin sister, came home from band practice, she read it too. Mom called my dad at his house in Pennsylvania, but they were both unsure of what to do. Mom threatened to go to the principal if I didn't let her call Marcy and Crystal's mothers, but Dad and I feared that reporting the girls for bullying or confronting their parents would make things worse. I wanted to switch middle schools, but Caitlin said that transferring meant the Haters had won.

I began to obsess over what made me so unlikable. Was it the way I danced at school dances (arms stiff like a robot), the old-lady phrases I used ("That's a sin!"), or the way I dressed (Mom jeans and baggy polo shirts)? I knew I was dorky (I had unruly sideburns and an overbite), but I had spent so much of seventh grade trying to change my image, to make new friends, to transition smoothly from elementary school to middle school.

Other kids became meaner once they found out I had received the Hate Note. A girl named Tina would prank phone call my house in the middle of the night, a boy named Bobby would flinch and yelp whenever I came near him, and a girl named Priscilla, who sat behind me in social studies, would fart and then blame me.

I tried to act indifferent, but it was difficult not to cry. Having Caitlin in school helped, but we rarely interacted—she was in the "smart" track, which gave us opposite and separate schedules, and she was nerdy too. What more could she have done for me?

Eventually I stopped talking in school, except when a teacher forced me to answer a question or work with a partner, but even then I spoke little.

When seventh grade ended, I spent the first half of summer in my room journaling or listening to the *Evita* soundtrack, preferring the songs about society's rejection of Eva Perón. My parents eventually forced me to go outside, to spend time with Caitlin. We went down the shore, got water ice at the strip mall, watched movies at the two-dollar movie theater—we had fun. By the end of the summer, I felt better, but I was far from fixed.

On the first day of eighth grade, I stood in the cafeteria and faced the ultimate first-day dilemma: where to sit during lunch.

Almost everyone hated me, according to the note, so I scanned the cafeteria for the girl with the olive complexion, shoulder-length wavy brown hair, blue braces, and long, slim face. My twin. The cafeteria noise grew, as if a maestro had raised his baton and directed everyone to talk louder, and the room smelled like french fries. My foot was just about to pivot toward the exit sign when I finally found Caitlin sitting at the opposite end of the table.

I walked up and stood behind her. She sat hunched over a fraction worksheet and tapped the tip of her nose with the end of a pencil. For Caitlin, looking at a math problem was like looking at the face of God. Our thirteen years together had taught me that interrupting a math savant would be like sticking my arm into the mouth of an alligator, but she was my closest ally, my saving grace.

"Hey. Can I sit with you?"

"Duh!" Caitlin said. "Hey, can you slide down?" she asked the kids who sat on the same bench as her. Everyone moved closer together until a spot opened up next to Caitlin. I sat down and smiled quickly at her, then dumped all the contents from my brown paper bag onto the table. Caitlin shoved her worksheet into her backpack and patted my back while looking down at her lunch, which was a peanut butter and jelly sandwich cut into four equal pieces. She ate one-fourth of it and leaned in close to me. "Welcome to our table," she whispered.

I pretended to wipe sleep from my eye to block a tear from falling. Of course she would let me sit with her—although she had a moral, familial obligation to be my friend, I knew we were *actual* friends, no matter what DNA or womb we shared—but having no other option made me feel like a loser. I thanked her and waited for someone to throw a handful of fries at me or hiss like a grumpy cat, but nothing happened.

While others discussed their summer vacations, I stared at the bleached-blond bangs of the girl in front of me. They were brighter than the sun, but the rest of her hair was brown. Except for the bangs, we looked similar, although my hair—brown like hers—was more knotty than frizzy. We both had round faces, but she had rosy, chubby cheeks, and mine were fat and freckled. I had Elvis sideburns, while hers were short and feminine. She resembled a quirky, chubby chipmunk. By this time I figured I must resemble a Vegas lounge gorilla.

"I'm Emma," the girl said. She held out her hand. It was the first time in a long time that someone other than Caitlin had reached out—literally or figuratively—to me. The gesture, though small, gave me hope.

"Lindsey," I said. I shook her hand, and then watched her stuff potato chips into her turkey and cheese sandwich. *Genius,* I thought.

"Not to be mean, but did you notice the mole on her forehead? I swear it had a heartbeat," Caitlin said to the girl next to her.

"Are you talking about Madame Saillard?" I asked.

"*Señora* Saillard," Caitlin said.

This was the first real conversation I had engaged in since walking through the school's doors at eight a.m. Maybe it was the comfort Caitlin provided me, Emma's friendly handshake, or the surge of some nutrition in my body, but I finally found my words.

"She's the worst!" I said. "I had her second period. She yelled at me in

French until I realized she was saying 'I'm a twin too,' and I was like, 'Oh, you must have met Caitlin.'"

"Foreign language teachers shouldn't be allowed to speak in a foreign language until the second day of school," Emma said.

"I agree," Caitlin said. She laughed, shook her head, and finished the remaining three-fourths of her sandwich.

"I was sitting behind you when that happened, and I thought, *Oh no, that sucks for her!* But you did a good job not freaking out and all," Emma said.

The bell rang, but I didn't want to leave. I had to say something to keep our conversation going, but I was rusty.

"What class do you have next?" I asked.

Emma and I compared schedules and realized that we had the same afternoon classes. While we walked to our next class, I wondered: Had she signed the Hate Note too? Her name didn't sound familiar. Still, I couldn't be sure.

We walked into English. Emma grabbed my arm and led us to two empty seats. The gesture felt strangely new, and yet it wasn't. Marcy had done the same thing the year before.

When I got home that day, I searched my room for the Hate Note. Piles of junk littered my bedroom floor. I tossed a bag of old clothes into the hallway, a bald Barbie over my shoulder, and stopped when I found a shoe box under a tower of baby blankets. I opened the lid, pulled out the crinkled notebook paper, skimmed through the list of names, and searched for Emma Germaine. She was nowhere on the list.

We were inseparable for the rest of the year. I learned that she loved *Saved by the Bell*, dotted her *i*'s with stars, obsessed over Hanson, suffered from chronic toe cramps, liked to wrestle with her brothers, thought her mom was kind of weird, and considered me one of her best friends.

Because we were best friends, I told her about the Hate Note. She had never heard of it, but called Marcy and Crystal "cowardly" and "cruel" for what they had done. Emma believed that dropping friends was "so dumb."

I agreed.

Two weeks after our deli date, I sat at my computer and stared at my empty MySpace in-box. Something felt wrong, so I called Emma and left a voice mail. She didn't call back. I texted—nothing. For the next year, I continued to call, text, and e-mail—I even wrote a four-page letter and delivered it to her mailbox—but Emma remained silent.

Years went by. I quit MySpace, my scoring job, and T-Word and became an English teacher. Adam and I rebuilt our relationship and got married. Although I still felt Emma's absence, I felt it less as the years passed—until 2012. Our ten-year high school reunion.

On the Friday after Thanksgiving I sat on my bed with a glass of red wine and ran my finger through my curls.

"Stop playing with it," Danielle said, slapping my hand away from my head. She stood on her tippy toes as she wrapped another strand of my hair around the curling barrel, squirted it with hairspray, and cursed the gods for making her so short.

"No more wine," Kat said. "You've had three glasses. I've only had one and I'm already feeling it. You don't want to be drunk tonight." She grabbed my glass and left the room.

"Are you nervous?" Danielle asked.

Danielle and Kat were my other best friends – and they had suffered through the Emma drama with me. They even memorized My Multiple Theories for Why Emma Dumped Me:

Theory 1: Hanson—no explanation needed.

Theory 2: I said something at lunch that made Emma think less of me. Maybe it was my disregard for Adam's feelings, how much I talked about myself, or the fact that I kissed someone named T-Word.

Theory 3: Emma squeezed all she could out of our friendship and started to find me irritating. She didn't know how to walk away from me slowly, so she ran.

Theory 4: Aliens. Aliens abducted Emma.

Theory 5: Too much chicken in my teeth.

The girls knew I had been dreading the reunion, but they also knew I had to go. Emma would be there. She had organized the event.

"I'm just trying to figure out how we pretend like we don't already know everything there is to know about these people," I said.

"Thanks for ruining our reunion for us, Facebook," Danielle said. "Okay, all finished." She fluffed my hair with her hands and gave it one last spray.

Kat said I looked "very Jersey." I put on a black blouse and red lipstick, which made me feel artsy. Adam walked by the door and whistled at me. I winked and blew a kiss.

"You need heels," Kat said. I kicked off my black flats and pulled out nude, patent-leather heels from the bottom of my closet. "No, not those," she said.

I crawled farther into my closet and came out with a pair of black lace platforms, which had a small peacock feather glued to the back of each shoe.

"Perfect," Kat said.

"They're a little too tall for me," I said. I tried to gain my balance as I stood in them, but the six-inch heel and rounded, chunky sole caused me to tilt forward.

"It doesn't matter. You look hot," Kat said. "We gotta go."

I ran into the dining room to grab my purse, tripped twice in my heels, listened to Adam's brief Emma lecture about character and bravery, kissed him good-bye, and left with the girls.

Danielle drove us to Philadelphia, where Emma had planned for our classmates to meet, despite the fact that we had graduated from a New Jersey high school. Kat talked about how smart we were for leaving the boys at home, and how awkward it would be to see her ex-boyfriends. Danielle told us about her latest baby ultrasound. We reminisced. I don't know why those things made me think of all the times I had called Emma crying, missing her, begging her to call me back, but they did. I felt ridiculous.

"But you had to keep contacting her," Kat said. "No one assumes that her best friend has dumped her."

"You know it's not your fault, right?" Danielle asked. I shrugged. "You two had your bad times, too. It wasn't all good," she said.

I realized that Danielle had a point. Emma and I had never been perfect. She'd made more time for Hanson than she had for me, and her weight loss had made me jealous and insecure. We rarely fought, but we *did* fight.

We pulled up to the bar, its neon lights blinking. I wondered why this, out of all places, would be the place Emma picked for our reunion. My forehead started to sweat.

"You okay?" Kat asked.

"Yes. I mean no. But yes," I said.

Danielle put her hand on my leg. "Babe, you're going to be fine," she said. "We're here with you."

We walked into the bar. Purple balloons hung from the ceiling, and two figures handed out name tags from behind a table. Kat grabbed mine and leaned down, her six-foot-two-inch body shadowing mine as her blond hair brushed my face.

"She's right there. Look up. Get it over with," she said.

There stood Emma. She wore a black racer-back tank top, black skinny jeans, and black ankle boots, and she was still slim, but her side-swept bangs were dark brown and the tips of her sleek hair were blond. She looked the opposite of the girl I once knew.

(I wasn't surprised. Emma didn't have Facebook, but some of her friends were my Facebook friends, and they occasionally posted photos of her. I often wondered if her friends viewed my page and told her about my life, which was why I posted with caution.)

Emma waved to me and mouthed out, *Hey.*

Hey, I mouthed back. I smiled a shaky smile and marched past her.

The girls and I mingled. People asked about Caitlin, who hadn't come because she assumed everyone would act fake. Every couple of minutes I looked for Emma. She stood with Crystal—Hate Note Crystal—whom she had befriended in high school ("She's nice now!"). While Danielle and Kat were in the photo booth, I ran to the bar, got a drink, and chugged it.

At some point in the night, I walked up to Emma as she chatted with a jock and tapped her on the shoulder.

"Can we talk for a second?" I asked. Wine made me bold.

"Sure, in a minute," Emma said.

In a minute? I thought. *In minute? How about right now? I've only waited five goddamn years.*

"Yeah, okay, no problem."

While Emma finished her conversation, I wandered around and ran into Lauren, whose hair looked like a combination of a lion's mane and a palm tree. She told me I looked much better than I did in high school, and I told her, in my slurred speech, that I heard she was a stripper.

"Kemp," Emma shouted. "Come here." She waved me over to her, and as I walked, I thought of all the things I wanted to ask: *How are you? What the hell happened? How many purgatory strikes do you have? And how are the fucking Hanson brothers?*

According to Kat, who watched us from a few feet away, Emma and I talked for a while, but I only remember parts:

Me: "Why did you stop talking to me?"

Emma: "Oh, Lindsey."

Me: "I thought we were best friends. I loved you. What did I do? Why do you hate me?"

Emma: "I don't hate you. Listen, we'll talk when you're sober, but I don't hate you."

I wanted to punch her for calling me drunk, but wanted to kick my own ass more. I rarely drank like this. How could I, after all these years, not be sober for this moment?

Emma: *(Grabbing my left hand and pulling it up to her face)* "I want to talk about this, Lindsey! You got married!"

Me: "I know. I married Adam."

Emma: "I know, I saw on Facebook."

That's when Drunk Lindsey said to herself, *She must have looked at my Facebook profile from a mutual friend's account! She must have been curious. She must have cared.*

Emma: "You were such a gorgeous bride. I'm so happy for you. Really."

Drunk Lindsey: *Should I hug her? I'm going to hug her.*

Me: "Thanks. So when I'm not drunk . . . not that I am . . . do you think we could talk?"

Drunk Lindsey: *She's hesitating. Abort the hug.*

Emma: ". . . Yeah. Sure."

She called my phone so that I could have her number, and then blank splotches fill the rest of the night. I do remember that after I talked to Emma, I ran to the bathroom and cried on my knees in the handicapped stall. I kept thinking, *You are a moron, you blew it, sober up, stop crying, stop letting her see you upset, let it go, no more questions, be cool,* but I couldn't be cool. Danielle and Kat made me open the stall door and held me as I begged them, in between sobs, to never leave me. They told me I was crazy to think they ever would.

And then, later in the night, I fell. Twice. In front of Emma.

"Oh, Lindsey, no," I remember Emma saying the first time I fell.

"It's these goddamn shoes," I said. She helped me up and Danielle handed me a glass of water.

Two minutes later, I fell again. It was such a slow fall that Emma had time to grab my glass of water out of my hand before I hit the floor.

That's all I remember.

The next day, I slept until four p.m. When I felt strong enough to sit up, I noticed that Adam had placed a cup of coffee and an egg sandwich next to me. I checked my phone. Sixteen unread text messages waited for me in my in-box, but none from Emma.

I mulled over My Multiple Theories for Why Emma Dumped Me. They were just theories, though. I could never be sure which one, if any, was true. Not unless I asked—again. I grabbed my phone, found Emma's number on my missed-call list, and sent her a text:

> *I'm sorry for being such a drunken asshole last night. And for falling. And for blaming my shoes. It was good to see you.*

Five minutes later, she shocked me with a response:

> *Awww ha-ha, don't worry about it. It was great to see you! And I really mean everything I said. Really, I do.*

Except I couldn't remember *everything* she had said. Some of it had vanished into the drunken black holes of my mind. I texted back:

> *I would love to get together and talk about stuff, if you ever want to. If you don't, that's fine too. I'll understand.*

I waited.

> *Sure. If that's what you want to do, I'm willing to do it. Text me in a couple of weeks and let me know when and where.*

A couple of weeks passed, and as they did, I tried to imagine what would happen if Emma and I did meet. I would ask her *why*, and she might answer. And yet every time I imagined her answering, my stomach tightened. Somewhere in our five years of silence a truth was hidden, and I was just now starting to understand: I wasn't upset because I missed Emma. I was upset because I still struggled with trusting my friends. So I never responded.

I still doubt myself, though. I still question my friendships. Could there be a sliver of truth in the silly words of two mean girls from seventh grade? For so long Emma said no—and then suddenly yes. Maybe my truth lies somewhere in the middle: maybe I'm an imperfect woman who is capable of friendship. It just takes a lot more time and effort to earn my trust. But I'm afraid I'll always be a little unsure, a little uneasy, waiting for the next friend to leave.

Lindsey Kemp is a Creative Nonfiction graduate student in the Stonecoast MFA in Creative Writing program at the University of Southern Maine. Her writing has appeared in Metropolis *and* 5x5, *and she blogs for* Quirk Books. *Lindsey loves all things purple, Conan O'Brien, Tina Fey, and cheese (which she isn't supposed to eat but does, despite the consequences). She teaches English at a middle school in New Jersey, where she lives with her ginger husband.*

Off the Line

Julie VanDeKreke

High school. Finally. Freshman year, new school, new girl. My parents had recently divorced, and my father and I moved from my childhood home to another part of the Chicago suburbs. My mother had left us for another man only a few months prior, and my father, left to raise me, was selling our family home to move into a cheaper duplex. It was all we could afford. I kept most of my childhood relics, including clothing. We had to hang on to what we had, since we didn't have that much.

New town, new school. New haircut, fresh new eyeliner, trying to fit into the eighties. I walk down an orange and black hallway, up one level, to my new locker, and she's there. Burning red hair, bright green eyes; half her bangs cover one eye and she's staring right at me with the other. I feel awkward, walking toward her, but I realize as I count along the lockers that I am nearing my own. *1234, 1236, 1238, 1240 . . .* I count silently, my vision skipping from one to the next, her gaze never leaving me. I slow to a stop, almost right where she stands. She acknowledges my presence.

"Which one are you looking for?" She doesn't take her eye off me; she doesn't smile.

"1244," I say to her, seeing where it is before she responds. It is right next to hers.

"I'm Tiffany," she says, "but my friends call me Tiff. What class are you in next?" She's now smiling, but it's a hardened smile. Not the kind of girl you'd mess with. I like her already.

"Spanish."

"Come on. I'm going down that hallway."

We walk away from the lockers, and I realize I never even tried my combination. I next see her after my third-hour class, when she hands me a note—*Call me tonight*—with her number. I call her that night, meet her by my locker the next morning, and in no time we are talking every day. Weeks go by, a couple of months, sharing our stories about boys, about virginity. We are swapping our tight jeans and our tank tops. I talk about my parents, about the divorce, and about living with my father. She also lives with her father. Both of our mothers had affairs and left our fathers. We already have so much in common.

It's now November, my birthday month, and I'll be fourteen. I invite her, and two of her other friends, Tina and Dawn, to my sleepover birthday party at my father's house. We go down to my basement, where I've planned a German chocolate cake and ghost stories, laid out sleeping bags. Tiff seems more interested in talking about sex and boys. "Did they do it? Does she even like him?" Tina and Tiff are best friends, with Dawn coming in a close second. Once again, we spend time talking about our families, our siblings, our divorced or broken households, and ourselves, finding things in common and building what I imagined might be lifelong friendships based on the similarities we shared. Or, so I thought.

The next day after the party, they invited me to my first teen dance club. Hours before, the girls decided we should all wear short skirts. For me, black and white stripes. My new friends, these beautiful and cool girls, I wanted so much for them to like me. Although we had so much in common, I often thought I still wasn't in their league. I still felt like a little girl about to emerge into a woman, and these girls already looked the part. I was determined to have them keep me in their group.

I didn't have the money to buy a new skirt, so I'd torn up an old one I'd had when I was a few years younger. I tried my best to fit in. My first kiss, his name was Bill, inside a phone booth, the girls daring me: "Go on, Julie, he's cool, he likes you." Not being able to dance but shaking it anyway.

My efforts, however, were sadly in vain. Dawn and Tina were the first to pull away. Day after day they began to exclude me in some way. At the lunch table by saying they were finished eating as soon as I would sit. Or they would meet at another place after we all agreed to meet outside at the benches, just so I would go searching for them and not be able to find them until later. Then they would give me a sad "Sorry for not seeing you," as in *Sorry for ditching you; we didn't want to hang out with you.*

But I persisted.

At last the girls made it final. They made it clear to me I wasn't popular enough, good enough, for their clique. They did it with a phone call. Three-way—one at Tina's house with Tiff leading the conversation, one with Dawn on the other end, calling me from another house.

"Julie?" Tiff said on the other end. "We are calling you because"—I could hear giggling—"because . . . we don't want to be your friend anymore. You're just not . . . you're kind of . . ."

"Kind of what?" As if I didn't know.

"You're just . . . not . . . cool enough. To hang with us. I mean, you're nice and all, and we can say hi to you once in a while, but you're just not fun to hang out with. You're not like us."

And just like that, I was *dumped*. Eliminated.

School was awkward after that. I'd see Tiffany in the hall and she'd just glare at me or slam her locker, and then walk away, suddenly laughing.

I felt as though I was alone in a sea of teenagers trying to survive this nightmare of life. First my mother leaving our family and now this. The girl I had so much in common with was now isolating me. I didn't understand what I had done wrong, and I wanted an explanation.

A few weeks after, I wrote her a letter. I passed it to her when she was leaving her locker one day, casually, hand to hand. She took it and walked away. It simply said:

What did I do so wrong for you guys to not want to be friends with me anymore?

Later, she found me at my locker again and handed me a response. She wrote back:

Because you're not cool.

So I thought it was over: the friendship, hanging out, dance clubs, new boys.

It should have been over then, but it wasn't.

Days later my phone rang. When I answered it, there was muffled laughing on the other end. "Hello?" I could hear two girls laughing.

Slam.

I put the phone back on the receiver. I knew it was a prank.

But the phone continued to ring again. And again. And again.

In fact, for three days straight into the weekend, my phone did not stop ringing from nine a.m. until midnight. Each phone call was usually the same: muffled laughter, and at times a small child, or a voice of one, would echo my saying "Hello?" Sometimes I would answer the phone and not say anything, and the laughter would begin regardless of my silence. Hours of taking the phone off the hook, only to hang it back up and have it ring within minutes. At times my father answered the phone, yelling that he was going to trace the number and call the police (there was no caller ID back then), only to have them laugh harder and call right back within seconds after he'd hung up.

Two girls laughing, sometimes three. A three-way prank call.

My father called the police, but they told him he needed to file a motion with the county court, and that the police alone could not do anything in their power to make the phone calls cease. He tried to use *69, a feature where an automated voice recites the last phone number to call you, and called the given number a few times. He even spoke to a woman who claimed to be Dawn's grandmother about the persistent phone calls, but no matter how many times he would intervene, the phone would only keep ringing and ringing.

My father said, "Julie, you need to stand up to those kids."

My father said it was the "principle of the thing."

"Can't we just change the phone number?" I would say to him, almost daily when the phone would ring and ring. He would go back to one word: *principle*.

"You can't let these kids push you around. Besides, it costs money to change a phone number," he would reply.

My father began working the night shift a few days later. I was alone to answer the phone. When it would ring, I wouldn't check who it was; I would pick it up and hang it back up, and then I would take it off the hook for the rest of the night.

That Monday at school, mindful of my father's request, I walked right up to Tiffany at her locker. Determined. She was glaring at me again, but it didn't stop me from confronting her. "Are you and your friends calling my house and hanging up?"

She seemed to give it some thought. "I don't think so."

I continued. "Look. It's one thing if you don't want to be friends and hang out, but please stop calling my house."

Innocently: "I'll ask the girls and get back to you."
She passes me a note after lunch.

*Dawn and Tina said they called a few times, but that's it. I asked
them to not call again.*

After school that Monday, within a half hour, the phone rings. It's them.
Of course. I hang up. They call again. I take the phone off the hook for
the rest of the night. And the next night after school. And the next. My
father isn't home. I began to lose sleep; I stop eating. And all throughout
the weekend, the phone won't stop ringing. My father is home then, and,
knowing that *69 costs a dollar and fifty cents each time, he refuses to use
it.

We both know who is calling. Who it is. And they won't stop.

Each day. Every hour. Every minute, in fact, or so it seems.

All week. And the next. My father calls their number a few more times,
asks to speak to someone, anyone who is an adult. This time, someone who
identifies herself as Dawn's mother picks up the phone. My father threatens
that he does not want to take action by having to go all the way down to
the courthouse to file a motion to make this stop, but he will—even though
he has already made it clear to me he will not. He wants me to stand up to
them all. He shouldn't waste his time spending money and hours off work
at the risk of losing his job to make this stop, and I don't blame him.

After that, the phone is silent for the rest of the evening, but the silence
doesn't last. It begins that next evening, when my father is working the
night shift and I am home alone, again.

I see them each day during school, snickering when I walk by, laughing.
I am their entertainment, their good time, their bully victim; they want to
beat me up by calling, by abusing me over the phone.

And it doesn't stop after two weeks. It keeps on; they keep on. The child's
voice, the laughter, ring upon ring upon ringing of the phone until finally,
one day, three weeks later, after the phone doesn't stop ringing and my
father isn't home to say, "Make it stop, Julie," I finally decide to do just that.
Make it stop.

It's two a.m. Saturday morning, and my father is gone on his last night
shift before the weekend. I know that the girls are likely to be hanging
out together, spending the night at Tina or Tiffany's. I know this, because

at some point throughout these many weeks I've figured out that Dawn's mom doesn't like it when Dawn has friends spend the night. Tiffany lives with her dad, who works all night, so the girls have the house to themselves. Tina lives with a single mom who works late and likes it when the girls are around. So the least likely house they will spend the night at will be Dawn's house.

I've also figured out that all the midweek phone calls are coming from Dawn's house while her mother is working. My father did in fact call the phone company and the police department and put a trace on the phone call to make it official. When we called the number to tell them we had the actual trace and we could take them to court, and the person who identified herself as Dawn's grandmother said she would talk to Dawn and ask her to stop. But Dawn insisted that she was not calling.

But it had continued. And again the police told my father to file a motion in court. And still my father didn't want to. He just wanted me to stand up to them. He just wanted it to stop. And so did I. Desperately.

I got dressed: jeans, tennis shoes, baseball cap, and jacket. Ponytail. Backpack. It was December, and cool outside.

I walked out of the house, quietly, and down the street. I decided to stop at Dunkin' Donuts for a doughnut and coffee. A disinterested woman working the counter didn't ask where I was going, or why I was out in the middle of the night with a backpack, looking like a runaway. I paid, thanked her, and was on my way.

It was suburbia, peaceful, the air crisp and clean. Nice neighborhoods, quiet neighbors—typical for this area. Exactly the thing you would expect so very early before people begin waking for their Saturday morning coffee and reading their morning newspapers, maybe a mom in the kitchen making a nicer kind of breakfast than on a regular day. The kind of morning teenagers sleep in until noon.

I arrived at my destination. The house was dim, the lights off. The streetlights were far enough away where I could slip right into the darkness. I had to wait for a few moments for my eyes to adjust in order to see exactly what I was searching for. And I knew exactly what it looked like. I'd asked my father a few days prior. Oddly, he hadn't asked why.

Finally, I spotted it. My heart pounding in my chest, I approached the side of the house, laid down my backpack on the ground, and took out what I had brought with me.

Wire cutters.

Feeling the phone line with my fingers against the house, a large, black wire, I did a quick snip; then placed the tool back into the backpack and walked quickly away. I looked back to see if anyone had noticed me; no one had. I felt the nervous sweat turn to coolness on my face as I walked farther and farther away from the house, back down the street, letting the December air move me, push me along.

It took me all of the rest of the walk home and reaching my front door to convince myself I wouldn't get caught. It was still dark when I arrived back home, and my father was still at work. As I crawled into bed, my heart was still pounding.

But I knew that this time, I would be the one to have the last laugh.

It was around three in the afternoon the next day when my phone rang. "Hello?" I answered, not faltering, composed. I wasn't sure if it would be them, but I was prepared, and I knew exactly what I would say if it was. In my mind, I noted it was several hours later than the usual morning wake-up prank call.

Laughter, muffled. A child's imitated voice on the other end, mimicking me. Only one voice this time, with another voice in the background. Interesting. They must be calling from another phone line.

"Hello?"

I don't skip a beat. "Dawn? Is this you?"

Giggling.

"Did you notice something wrong with your phone line today?"

Silence.

"Was it, like . . . cut?"

I smile.

I wait. Silence like death comes through the receiver. I wait for several more seconds, waiting for a response—a noise of any kind. The only thing I hear, for the first time since this all began, is the sweet sound of the other person hanging up the phone.

Shaking, but smiling, I put the phone, gently, down in the receiver and wait, anticipating the phone to ring again. Perhaps even waiting for her grandmother to call me, trying to get me to admit to it. Something.

But silence. Silence that day, that night, and the next day. Silence for the rest of the week. In the hallways, the girls look at me, not smirking, not laughing, but silent—sideways this time, wary, knowing that I've had my revenge for being dumped. For being dumped on. For being their bully victim. When they realized what I had done to Dawn's phone line, they knew they had to cover for it because they had carried on a lie with her grandmother about not calling. How could they turn me in?

I never told my father what I did until years later. I expected him to be mad, but I would say he was more shocked at first. Then after several minutes he laughed and said they had it coming to them. I think he was proud; he had wanted me to learn to stand up for myself. And the girls must never have told their parents, because no one ever said a thing afterward.

I never had another phone call from them, nor did I ever allow them to bully me again—nor anyone else, for that matter. I may have desperately wanted to fit in, but not at that price. Like my father said, it's the principle of the thing.

Julie Van De Kreke's work has been featured in Mused: BellaOnline Literary Review, the Southern Women's Review, Monkeybicycle, *and the* Pop Fic Review. *She currently lives in Colorado, where she teaches middle school language arts to aspiring young writers.*

High School Never Ends

Susan Cushman

As a sixty-three-year-old woman, I'm embarrassed to share my story being unfriended back in high school in 1966. It was my sophomore year (our school didn't include freshmen), and I was nervous about many things—academics, extracurricular activities, and especially popularity. Having been a cheerleader in junior high, I had set the squad as my top goal for high school, but it was one that eluded my grasp not only that first year but in the years to follow. I focused on other activities, keeping busy on the newspaper staff, in theater guild (both acting and creating sets with the advanced art class), and with student council. What became new avenues in my pursuit of popularity and success evidently alienated my best friends, the old group from junior high. And they weren't subtle about unfriending me.

It was a weekday in early September, that nodal sophomore year, when Cindy (not her real name) asked me to come by her house after school. We usually only hung out on weekends, which were filled with pep rallies, ball games, dances, and slumber parties. I wondered what was up when I pulled into her driveway and rang the doorbell. But I was optimistic—naive, one might say—figuring maybe she wanted my help planning a surprise party for one of our friends or something equally fun. I couldn't have been more wrong.

"I don't know how to say this," she began. "But some of us just don't want to hang out with you any more."

"What do you mean?" I could barely speak, as the lump in my throat grew bigger by the second. I felt light-headed. We were in Cindy's bedroom, where I had spent many happy sleepovers, but the room suddenly felt cold and threatening.

"It's just that you're all about trying to be popular, and we're not into that."

How does a fifteen-year-old respond to an affront like that? I had no tools for salvaging my self-esteem from such a direct hit. If there was more to the conversation, I can't remember it. It happened, after all, almost fifty years ago. I do remember crying my heart out for days before I gathered the courage to start looking for new friends.

Ironically, the group of girls who unfriended me went on to be part of the popular crowd—some were on the drill team; others finding success in arenas similar to mine (journalism, academics, student government, theater, music). I watched them pursue and achieve their goals each year, wondering what was different about the way we were living our lives. Why had I been singled out as the only one whose fragile adolescent ego sought survival through wanting to be popular and successful? How was their pursuit of those same things acceptable? It was doubly ironic that the new group of friends I cultivated wasn't part of that top tier of the most popular and successful kids. None of us were cheerleaders, members of the drill team, or girlfriends of athletes.

High school finally over, I entered my freshman year at the University of Mississippi. On the surface things continued to go well. My sorority sisters elected me as president of the pledge class. At the end of that year I married one of the "cool kids" from Ole Miss. Bill was in a top fraternity. He was even president of the senior class. He was headed to medical school back in Jackson on a full scholarship. One would think I "had it all" and my adolescent insecurities would have dissipated. But somehow I seemed to carry them with me into the early years of our marriage. I was always waiting for the other shoe to drop.

The years went by, and suddenly it was time for our ten-year high school reunion. I attended with my husband, hoping that the cliquishness of high school would have faded and everyone would have grown up. Incredibly, those hurtful vibes were still in the air, so I chose not to attend our twenty- and thirty-year reunions. Then 2009 rolled around and we were all close to turning a mature sixty. Over the last few years I had run into a number of classmates on visits to my hometown, and they had seemed genuinely glad to see me. One asked if I was coming to our forty-year reunion that summer. I decided to give it another try.

Several of the girls in that original group of my closest friends were at the reunion and welcomed me with smiles and hugs. A couple of them lived in different states, but a few more had returned to our hometown. They invited me to have lunch with them on my next visit.

The luncheon was fun—full of stories of our lives since high school. I was a bit wary not to talk too much about any "successes" I'd had, in case they might think I was all caught up in being "popular." Again. It felt good just to be accepted, and I agreed to meet for lunch again soon. It was during our next visit that I would strap my courage on and confront Cindy about what happened back in 1966.

Why was it still so important to me? A therapist's wisdom was helping me understand the residual effects of this wound, especially when coupled with childhood sexual abuse and a lifetime of verbal and emotional abuse at the hands of my mother. Victims of abuse often have self-esteem issues. Mine had plagued me for decades, surfacing in eating disorders and addictive behaviors. I had learned much about confronting and/or forgiving my abusers, but these girls from my teenage years still had some kind of emotional hold on me.

Maybe it was a bad decision to ask Cindy about that event some forty years in the past. I wasn't trying to embarrass her, but I needed help moving on. The table grew silent as I recalled the incident. I looked into Cindy's eyes and said, "It might seem silly now, but I just need you to know how much that hurt me." I held my breath, waiting for her apology. It never came.

"Susan, I don't remember that at all."

Her words felt like a knife cutting open an old wound. I immediately tried to save face as everyone picked up their wineglasses and looked uncomfortably around the restaurant—anywhere but at me.

"Really? Well, it was a long time ago and we were just teenagers." There I sat, decades later, still waiting, still hoping. My hope died as someone changed the subject, and it was never revisited. I haven't been invited back to lunch with those friends since that day.

While researching this essay, I was darkly comforted by the universality of what I had lived through in stories like "Why We Never Get Over High School" (The Atlantic, February 2014) and "Why You Truly Never Leave High School" (New York Magazine, January 2013). And then I read the wiki article "How to Get over Being Unfriended on Facebook." Some of the reasons listed caught my attention:

Are you showing off?
Are you trolling for praise?
Do you overshare?
Ouch. I love Facebook. When I joined in 2009, I had already been blogging for two years. I saw Facebook as a place to network with other writers and folks in the publishing world. And yes, I always link to my blog posts on Facebook (and Twitter) to draw more traffic to my site. Is that being superficial? Showing off? Doesn't everyone do that? Doesn't it help to build the sense of community we all long for?

I discovered the joy of keeping up with friends (both old and new) in faraway places, and Facebook became for me—a writer who works in solitude—a social-media haven.

I've forgiven the girls who unfriended me in high school, but Cindy's words will always be with me. And maybe that's not a bad thing, if I can use them to become a more authentic person without going all introspective in a navel-gazing way. Maybe I *was* being superficial in my approach to finding happiness. I know now that my wounded teenage psyche was doing the best it could to survive what might be the most difficult of all life stages. Maybe we never do get over high school.

Susan Cushman was Co-Director of both the 2010 and 2013 Oxford Creative Nonfiction Conferences and Director of the 2011 Memphis Creative Nonfiction Workshop. She was a panelist at the 2013 Louisiana Book Festival and the 2012 Southern Festival of Books in Nashville, and a speaker at the 2012 Creative Nonfiction at the Crossroads workshop in Clarksdale, Mississippi. She lives in Memphis. Susan is seeking agent representation for her novel, Cherry Bomb, *which made the short list for the 2011 Faulkner-Wisdom Creative Writing Competition. Her essays have been published in* The Shoe Burnin': Stories of Southern Soul *(River's Edge Media, 2013),* Circling Faith: Southern Women on Spirituality *(University of Alabama Press, 2012), and numerous journals and magazines. She blogs at www.susancushman.com/blog-pen-palette.*

Breaking Omertà

Alexandria Goddard

Editor's note:

Sixteen-year-old high school student "Jane Doe" was raped in August of 2012, at a party, by two other students, athletes, in the football town of Steubenville, Ohio. She was unconscious at the time. The rape and degradation were documented by party-goers on their cell-phone cameras and the photos went viral. Crime blogger Alexandria Goddard, who had once lived in Steubenville, brought it to national attention on her blog and was instantly vilified and discredited, as described in this article by Katie Baker from www.jezebel.com, "We Wouldn't Know About the Steubenville Rape Case if it Wasn't for the Blogger Who Complicated Things".

The Steubenville story, in all its complications, was picked up by the New York Times, 20/20, Dr. Phil ("Football, Booze and Bad Behavior," 1/17/13) and later by Rolling Stone in the article "Anonymous vs. Steubenville" by David Kushner, on 11/27/13. In April of 2014, Brad Pitt bought the rights to make a movie about Deric Lostutter, a member of the hacker collective Anonymous, who along with Goddard had originally pushed this story beyond the small-town attempts at cover-up and into the national consciousness.

Some might say the whistleblowers have been judged and treated more harshly than the rapists themselves. Much of the town considers itself the "Big Red Nation," the fan base of the football team in a town that has fallen on hard times and has little else for residents to affiliate with. At the time of this writing, Lostutter faces more jail time than the convicted boys. Goddard has been sued, and her reputation and safety have been repeatedly threatened, as she describes in the blog post on her site: prinniefied. blogspot.com, 1/14, Why Steubenville Matters.

And she was betrayed by one of her oldest friends. As a preface to her essay about this friendship, I interviewed Goddard:

Alexandria, I started following you when you were speaking out against the injustices of the rape case in Steubenville. When you spoke of losing friends because of your commitment to bring national attention to this crime, I knew I had to have you in my book. What prompted you to take this risk?

What prompted me to take the risk was the absolute outrage I felt at some of the online discussion regarding Jane Doe, which started almost a week prior to the arrest of the two juveniles. I was disgusted at some of the comments being made about the victim, and the number of individuals who immediately began making accusations that the only reason this was an issue was because it involved Steubenville High School athletes. It seemed everyone in town was talking about this, and the chain of events was documented on Twitter, yet no one had called the police themselves to report it. It was only reported after Jane Doe's family was made aware of the online evidence. The absolute absence of bystander intervention shocked me, and the victim blaming tore at my heart.

You speak in your essay of the code of silence, the omertà, but did you ever think that it would ever happen that your friends would turn on you?

I always felt that I was taking this risk, but I thought that those who knew me would not be surprised, as I was always someone who voiced my opinion—whether it was the popular one or not. I was honestly very surprised when I started seeing posts online directed to me from people that I once considered close friends.

As I reread these articles and blog posts describing what you went through, I am struck by how much the attacks on you parallel how quickly the public jumps to condemn and blame the victims in cases such as this. I wonder to what degree that affected you?

The online attacks by family and friends of the "Big Red Nation" have been very traumatic at times. Not only have I been maligned and harassed, but also my family has been subject to bullying, and worse, as I talk about in my essay.

There is a parallel regarding victim-blaming and condemning the victim for speaking out. The actions of those who victim-blame and condemn others who speak out are based on the desire to silence voices that refuse to be silent.

Who besides the friend you write about in the essay—let's call her Kathy—dumped you? Was Kathy the worst? The least expected?

Yes, Kathy was the worst. There were two others who were equally as shocking—especially an older woman who I was once very close to. I looked up to her and valued her opinion as an elder. Both of their behaviors were very hurtful. There are a few anonymous Twitter accounts who claim to be family of some of the boys, who they claim were "innocent." They have made it a point to use intimidation. One account had a profile banner that used my nickname and said *Run Prinnie Run.* When Kathy posted my address on Twitter, I was absolutely shocked and as a result packed the car and my two dogs and headed for Ohio. I have come to the realization that allowing them to intimidate me gives them power, and I have decided that I don't care if they know where I am. They would be really stupid at this point to try to harm me.

What other losses did you experience as a result of what I would consider true bravery on your part?

I left California in a terror. That to me is the ultimate loss, because I loved the desert. I do plan on moving back to the desert eventually.

Can you tell us about the lawsuit and the silencing? You do not seem a woman easily silenced.

When I was sued for defamation of character, I was advised by counsel to stop speaking about the case and not to do interviews. I still used Twitter, but I didn't speak of the case. It was difficult to do because I had *a lot* to say about the Saltsmans [the family of one of the tweeters who posted photos of the victim, but was not one of the rapists] trying to silence people about the case.

You were mentioned in an article in Rolling Stone about Brad Pitt optioning to buy the Steubenville story. What is new with that? And did you ever think you would be connected to a Brad Pitt project?

I have not had any conversations with Brad Pitt or Plan B Entertainment.

I never in a million years would have believed this case would have the social impact that it has. I always thought that this would end up a Lifetime movie, but never dreamed that Brad Pitt would be interested in the story. I hope that bystander intervention becomes a discussion in the movie, as I believe educating the public to be an "upstander" rather than a bystander is very important.

Has there been any reconciliation with Kathy or any of the others?

No, there has been no reconciliation. With all that Kathy has done, I'm not sure that I could ever consider her a trusted friend again. I don't hate her, but I realized that I obviously have nothing in common anymore with the person that she has become, and I'm okay with that.

Would you do it again?

Absolutely. I will never stop standing up for what I believe in. It's my nature. Sometimes it doesn't make me a very popular person, but I'm okay with that, too.

Breaking Omertà

Betrayal is a difficult emotion to put into words. Someone gets pissed off at you and throws a knife in your back. That's the quick and easy explanation, but how do you describe in words how that makes your heart feel? The initial shock when you are betrayed quickly turns into a feeling of heart-wrenching and heavy sadness, followed by an infinite stream of questions that begin with *why*.

Revenge was never my intention, nor did I have a grudge against the entire town when I blogged about the Steubenville rape case. I have been accused of that, and accused of hating the Big Red football program. All of this is ridiculous and a diversion. I wrote about the case because I saw locals online maligning Jane Doe and blaming her for her own rape. The local media didn't provide the social-media evidence that I found. People wanted and needed to know what was going on. They were trying to separate rumor from fact, and it was then that I decided to publish the now-notorious screenshots from social media from that night. I knew it would bring attention to the beloved high school football program, and that would upset a lot of people, but I never expected the vitriolic backlash that I have endured for over a year and a half. Especially from those I have called friends.

Many people, whom I once thought very highly of, turned against me for breaking *omertà*—the communal code of silence that dictates what is said aloud about certain people or situations. There is an old saying: "What happens at home stays at home." This is how I feel about life in Steubenville. There are things and people of whom thou shalt not speak. Nothing has changed in this regard since I left Steubenville almost twenty years ago.

When I lived in Steubenville, my best friend was Kathy. She was fun. She was not afraid to speak her mind and had an infectious laugh. I met her when I was dating a Steubenville police officer. His roommate was her boy-friend, who was also a police officer. We quickly became best friends after we met. For the sake of allowing this former boyfriend of mine to remain anonymous, I will call him Ace. He had his name tattooed on his leg.

Kathy dated Ace's roommate, and eventually married him. Kathy and I were the gruesome twosome and there was never any animosity or drama between us. She was my best friend, and for a time she lived with me. I was her maid of honor when she married her husband. For the time that we hung out, we were for the most part inseparable. Where you saw one, you saw the other.

After I moved away from Steubenville, we lost touch. As with many friendships, we went on about our own lives and grew apart. This wasn't an intentional distancing. She was married and starting a family and I was off doing my own thing. As I said, I don't ever recall any drama between us. Drama between the boyfriend and me—*absolutely*! But there were no issues with Kathy.

Ace hated that we hung out together, and he had a particular dislike for Kathy because she wasn't afraid to tell him how it was. She was just as stubborn as he was, and their coexistence was like oil and water. He and I had a very tumultuous relationship as well, built on beer and arguments. When Ace and I would break up—which was often—Kathy and I would hit a few of our favorite watering holes to laugh and just have fun. It was hysterical knowing that it pissed him off to no end that I was out partying when he had just dumped me. I suppose in his mind I was supposed to be at home bemoaning my lost catch? *Pffft*. I had my best friend, and we had some good times that made for even better stories.

Ace never called me by my name. He called me Goofy. I have no clue why he did, only that it was a huge joke amongst our circle of friends the way he said it. He had a deep and locally accented voice. Regional slang like "yinz" and "nibby" was a regular part of his repertoire, and with his tone it was just amusing to hear him growl, "Goofy."

One particular night Kathy and I went out, and as she and I were sit-ting at the bar with another friend, laughing and joking, Ace came in. He walked up to us, and it was pretty clear he wasn't pleased that we were all having a good time. I guess I'd forgotten to cry in my beer bemoaning the fact that we were broken up for the *eleven-billionth* time that month. Needless to say, my jovial mood didn't sit well with him. It was enough to cause that one vein on his forehead to pop out.

I looked at Kathy, she looked at me, and I will never forget when Ace looked at both of us. In his gruff voice he pointed to each of us, one at a time, to deliver his usual sentimental message filled with expletives and scorn. With a finger point, and a pause at each grinning face, he declared to each of us in succession: "Fuck you, fuck you, and *triple fuck you*, Goofy!" Of course, we all went hysterical with laughter that just annoyed him even more. He ranted and we laughed harder. It was a moment that went down in my history with Kathy and got more than a few gales of laughter over the years. The story became an obligatory part of our catching-up conversations, because it was just *that* funny.

Friendships withstand the test of time. People may move on in their own direction, but true friends will always pick up where they last left off, and that's how it was at first with Kathy. When I left Steubenville for greener pastures, she and I kept in touch on and off. It wasn't until I moved back to the Ohio Valley ten years later, and after my second back surgery, that we reconnected via Facebook. We picked right up.

I was having complications from a spinal fusion. After exhausting my medical leave I lost my job and moved into my brother's home while I recovered. During the time I was under medical care, my physicians prescribed heavy narcotics, and I became physically addicted to them. I'd had no clue this was even possible. You don't think of becoming addicted when you are taking medications properly. Addiction means that you are abusing meds, right? No. Anyone can get addicted to opiates, and very easily over a very short time.

I ended up in the ER, and when I realized that I was physically addicted, I freaked out. I didn't want to have anything controlling my life but me. After consulting with physicians and a substance-abuse counselor, I decided that I was going to detox myself . . . at home. I didn't want to wait for a bed to open up in a rehab two months later. I confided in Kathy about this. She is a health care professional, and I had asked her about complications of not doing this in a facility.

I detoxed cold turkey, and for three weeks I was sicker than I have ever been in my life. It was and is the most excruciating experience of my life. There were times that I begged to die because I was so sick. I cried. I couldn't move because I was so nauseous. I couldn't eat because I couldn't keep anything down. I couldn't even talk on the phone. I had seizures. I barely had the energy to crawl up the stairs to the bathroom, but I was determined to end my body's need for opiates. I listened to music on my iPod and would turn it up as loud as it would go because at least then my brain was thinking about something other than the excruciating feeling of "dope sickness" and withdrawal. I would listen to "Good Feeling" by Flo Rida over and over, because the chorus took me away from the pain and I wanted to be any-where in the world besides in that bed. Kathy stayed in touch, showed her concern, but there was not much anyone could do. I just had to wait it out.

Three weeks and a thousand tears later, my body was no longer depen-dent on prescription narcotics. I got through it, and like everything else that has happened in my life, it may have been very uncomfortable, but it made me a stronger person. Why am I telling you about this? It was something very private to me, and I confided in Kathy because she was my friend and friends disclose this type of information. I wasn't embarrassed to tell her what was going on, but later I would come to the horrible real-ization that my trusting disclosure would be used against me.

After the Steubenville case gained international attention, several Twitter accounts were created that did nothing but attack me and everyone associated with me. The people behind these pseudonyms were going to punish me for speaking out, and no one was off-limits—even my deceased father. My mother was called a whore and accused of bestiality. Pictures of me were photoshopped wearing a Nazi uniform because I am a German citizen. They swore that they were going to have me deported and that I should go to jail because as an immigrant they felt that I was not entitled to the same constitutional rights as they were as US citizens. These people were even trying to determine the identity of my biological father in Germany. Kathy's mother posted that she hoped I would get AIDS and die. They posted tweets that said God had punished me for being a horrible person and that's why I couldn't have children. Kathy's friends even posted pictures of my boyfriend, who was a Marine, and asked people to iden-tify him so they could contact his command to tell them what a horrible person he was dating. Then the accounts started tweeting about my "drug problem" and mentioning my brother.

I didn't know these people. How could they know about my personal life? And then it hit me. Kathy! It was a punch in the gut. I was literally sick to my stomach. My "friend" who was angry that I wrote about Steubenville had betrayed my confidence and used the things I shared with her as a way to retaliate. I was crushed. Not because these unknown individuals were harassing me and making false accusations that I was a "drug-abusing scumbag," but because my dear friend had shared the information with others for their bullying pleasure. She had also posted my address. I had been taking great care in keeping my location closely guarded because I had already received threats.

Nothing was off-limits to Kathy and her friends as long as they could use it to hurt me or the people I cared about. They soon targeted a dear friend who suffers a mental illness from severe childhood trauma. Every day this friend struggles to find the balance between being able to cope and avoiding triggers that cause her to spiral into rages. Her world is not an easy one, and Kathy and her friends took every opportunity to taunt her and exploit her illness. They were intent on punishing anyone associated with me, or anyone who was vocal against the rape that occurred in Steubenville. It wasn't enough, just trying to ruin me.

How do you recover from this type of betrayal? Most people would say you can't. But I have. I feel sorry for Kathy that she chose to jump on that passing wagon, using my trust in her as a means to validate her existence with the other haters. I never lashed out at her publicly. I never broke her confidence. Instead, I sat by and watched as she attempted to destroy anyone that I cared about just to get back at me for speaking my mind and pointing out an injustice, and speaking the truth about our town.

She isn't the only friend who turned on me for my role in the Steubenville case, but her rejection is the one that hurt the most. Life goes on, I did the only thing my conscience would allow, and rather than hang on to the hurt, I prefer to remember the good times, the important choices, and let it go at that.

Alexandria Goddard is the creator and editor of Prinniefied.com and is noted for breaking the Steubenville, Ohio rape case story. She has worked for over twenty years as a legal assistant with experience in fraud analysis and risk management. She is a former volunteer guardian ad litem-court appointed special advocate for the juvenile court system and the owner of Xander Business Group, Inc. which provides consulting services based around the profiling and monitoring of jurors, witnesses, and testimony impeachment, using social media as an investigative tool in the legal process. She has donated hundreds of hours to educators and others to promote awareness of bystander intervention, and assists veterans groups in the investigation of military stolen valor.

Literary Lessons and a Circle of Crones: The Evolution of a Women's Group

Elayne Clift

"Old age is no place for sissies."
—Bette Davis

There are among us one uterus, three ovaries, multiple husbands, current lovers, numerous children and grandchildren, and interesting careers. Two of us are cancer survivors. Another has a chronic disease. One has been sexually abused. We know better than most that Bette Davis was right.

That's why we have proudly called ourselves Crones for the twenty years we've been together—wise women of a certain age who have transitioned into the third stage of our lives with grace, spirited intelligence, humor, and a sense of belonging in this world. We are no longer what Simone de Beauvoir called "the Other," nor do we suffer Betty Friedan's "problem that has no name." Rather, we have lived at the center of our lives—not because we sport large egos, but because we understand the gifts that have been granted to us, and because we cherish the centrality of connection to others, and to the larger world, as we travel the life span.

Most people think of Crones as haggard, wizened women who have nothing to offer but remnants of memory. But in pre-patriarchal times, postmenopausal women were revered for their intellectual and spiritual gifts. Their counsel was sought by others because they were Wise Women. Healers and leaders, they were called upon at every occasion from birth

43

to death, where they exercised the benevolent power of the ancient tribal matriarch.

I learned about Crones, and the three archetypal stages of women's lives, as I was creeping up to my fiftieth birthday in 1993 and wondering how I would mark the event. I decided to have a Croning Celebration—sharing with special friends, women I'd known through the important phases of my life, celebrating my own passage past that milestone which so many others seemed to dread. I didn't want to do anything bizarrely New Age; I just wanted to have a good time with a great group of women with whom I had shared significant parts of my life.

And so, on a windy weekend in March, six middle-aged women and I headed for the beach to spend three days laughing, eating, drinking, walking, networking, all in no particular order. We've been Croning together ever since. This year marks our twentieth anniversary (and the start of our seventieth birthdays).

By the end of that weekend, the feast of friendship, female strength, pathos, and humor—all part of the celebration of women's lives—was deeply embedded in our collective psyche. We had shared much: boundless wit, the wisdom of age, occasional tears, a few extra pounds, adventurous spirits, and joy in our femaleness. We would be bonded forever.

I knew, of course, that my friends would like one another, and that my Croning Celebration would be special. What amazed me was the incredible connection that occurred among us in so short a time. And so it was that by the end of the weekend, amid hugs of farewell, we determined to do it again. We've now been traveling together for two decades, meeting about twice annually in places as diverse as the Caribbean, the Canadian Rockies, and the Grand Canyon. Once, my husband asked, "What do you *do* when you're together all that time?" We've talked, laughed, shared, celebrated milestone birthdays and new romances. We've counseled one another about the challenges we've continued to face as parents and partners. We've consoled the one among us who became widowed and the two of us who've been ill. We've worried about growing older.

Twenty years have now passed, and until recently I thought we were absolutely there for one another, closing ranks, no matter what kind of support was required. These women were my sisters and my soul mates. My chosen family. Individually and together, it seemed to me, we understood the beauty and necessity of female friendship and solidarity. We believed that each of us was larger in life than we would be without one another and that without any one of us, we would all be diminished. Because we had one another, each of us felt centered, balanced, whole.

Not long ago I penned a poem that began like this:

She awoke, and wondered again,
how many days would pass
before the sound of the slap
was no longer her rising image.
She thought it sounded like
the Titanic crashing into that iceberg,
the rapid snap tearing her in two
like the bow of the once indestructible ship.

Most readers would assume this is a poem about marital violence. In fact, the assault I wrote about came not from my spouse but from a Crone, a friend whom I'd loved and trusted for fifty-five years.

It began when we were sharing a meal together one balmy evening, in a place of tropical fruit and palm trees where we'd been meeting annually with our spouses for years. Suddenly something I said set her off, and she jumped out of her chair, spewing a vitriolic verbal attack. Screaming at me, so enraged that her face distorted into that of someone going mad, she shouted, "Can't you watch what you say? You're so dysfunctional! Don't you get it that's why all your friends leave you?"

Coming from someone who had valued me for five decades, a friend who had sought my advice and opinion, the accusation hit hard. I felt as if I'd been punched in the solar plexus, had the breath knocked out of me. The charge that I drove people away was stunningly cruel, because my friend knew how deeply I continued to grieve the loss of two close friends who had simply walked away from my life after years of intimate friendship, abandoning our connection as if I were so much detritus in the darkness of events that had impacted their own lives.

I wept long into the night after my friend's assault. The next morning I told her we were leaving. She leaped out of her chair, flailing her arms. I stumbled back as she pushed and shoved me, screaming, "Good riddance! Get the hell out!"

To understand the trauma of this event it's important to know this about my friend: She was the world's nicest person. Gentle and passive, she was someone I had teased for fifty-five years about how often she apologized when no apology was required. I had never heard her swear or say an unkind word about anyone. So what was going on?

The Crone I confided in about what had happened, a woman who has known both of us for over fifty years, conjectured marital problems, the pain of a torn meniscus, and other possibilities. I thought there must be pathology similar to the onset of the kind of dementia her mother had suffered.

And so my poem concluded:

Later, when she knew that the
fissure was not of her making,
but had come from a fractured, frail mind,
she rejected anger, replacing it with stoic silence.

But the sting was there, still and forever,
their long affection now on life support.
And having neither the courage nor the will
to pull the plug, she simply endured her loss,
quietly and alone, awaiting the next blow.

The thing is, although I'd never been verbally abused or physically assaulted before, it was not the first time someone I had loved and trusted totally with my interiority—my "inviolable self," as Willa Cather called it— had betrayed my faith in the power and pleasure of such deep friendship.

The first time it happened, my best friend in the world, someone with whom I'd made a profound connection the instant we met, stopped communicating. This woman had become my soul mate through the kind of friendship one is lucky to experience once in a lifetime. I saw her through her divorce and a series of disastrous professional dramas; she was with me when my sister, my brother, and then my mother died within three years. When she was sick, I was there. Whenever I was in despair, she was by my side.

Then she moved away for a new job that didn't work out. Withdrawing into somatic depression, she seemed to metamorphose into someone I no longer knew. Our phone conversations, which I initiated, grew increasingly one-sided and impersonal. I began to feel that she endured talking to me as if it were an uncomfortable obligation rather than the exchange we'd both hungered for and enjoyed over the past decade. Gradually the phone calls ceased and one-liner e-mails followed, until they too dissipated when I could no longer do all the heavy lifting of a relationship that seemed comatose at best. On the occasions when I did reach out, I felt pathetically needy as I tried to understand what had gone wrong and how our connection might be salvaged. Then I stopped. "When only one person is speaking," I wrote, "it isn't friendship. It's a humiliating gesture from someone pleading to be relevant."

Not long after that lost friendship broke my heart, someone else with whom I'd formed a strong mutual bond led to more pain. The woman was my graduate student. She was from an Asian country where my husband and I had worked and for which we felt a strong affinity. She and I bonded immediately over our mutual affection for her birthplace.

After her graduation and marriage our friendship deepened, growing into a relationship we agreed constituted "family." From the time her child was born, we shared Christmas holidays as what we laughingly called "People of the Book": a Jew, a Christian, and three Muslims. We stayed often in their home, where the overripe bananas I love were always present and the curry my husband relishes bubbled on the stove when we arrived. Then, suddenly, my "adopted daughter" stopped talking to me, just as my friend had done. She seldom returned my calls or e-mails, and when we did speak, she was cold in a way that stunned me. I wrote to ask what had happened. I went to see her so that she would look me in the eye and answer my simple question: Why? But there was no response.

What happened? I still don't know. I can speculate that since she stopped talking to me when her mother died, perhaps she was angry that I, her substitute mom, still lived. Perhaps she was debilitated by the depression I know she struggled with, a depression that made her withdraw into her own cultural community and away from American life.

The impact of these losses—my birth family, my best friend, and my "adopted daughter"—can only be described as nuclear winter. The terrain on which I lived became rocky and inhospitable, shaky, devoid of color and cool breezes to soothe a fragile soul. Although flowers grew there and I was blessed with my own family, the Crones, other friends, and even some new "adopted kids," I often felt alone in the world. I knew well the "solitude of self" Elizabeth Cady Stanton wrote about in late life. I developed fewer expectations about what friendship might hold, and held onto every suspicion that, given enough time, more would be offered than was received.

After my friend accosted me, I revisited the other losses, a reprise so powerful that it flooded my heart with renewed grief. I wept but did not sleep. I replayed scenes I'd long tried to retire. I composed verse and prose in my head that never made it onto the page. I seemed unable to recover from the multitude of wounds that had reopened in me. I suppose if I were to allow a label to be placed upon my suffering, it would be PTSD.

And then there is this: the wounds have another related history. Freud would say of them that they stem from "the absent mother." He would be right.

When I was seven years old, my beloved mother suffered her first "nervous breakdown." Labeled with "involutional melancholy," "manic depression," and other psychiatric jargon of the day, she suffered frequent hospitalizations that included humiliating, inhumane, ineffective treatments meted out by patriarchal physicians who knew nothing of failed marriages and the silencing of brilliant women. As a result my mother was more absent than present in the years of my growing up. I missed her terribly. The pain of her absence, her "abandonment," has never quite left me. That is part of the reason I chose to expose myself, never anticipating what followed.

I had decided it was necessary to share with the Crones what had happened between my old friend and me when we next met. It was, I felt, a matter of caretaking—of me in the immediate aftershock, and quite likely later of our friend, who was not present at that Croning. Also, I did not feel safe sharing a room with her again, as we had always done on our trips, and I needed them to understand for future reference. And so I found my courage and, hyperventilating, said, "I have something to tell you. It is not easy to hear, and not easy to tell. It's about something that happened when T. and I were together."

"Wait!" one Crone interrupted. "If this is going to be something that makes me choose between you two, I don't want to hear it!"

I was stunned. She had known me for twenty-five years. Did she really think I would stoop to that?

What followed as I tried to share my trauma was stunning, so out of the realm of what I had hoped for in the way of support that I could barely continue. As I related what had occurred, attention quickly focused on what might have made T. behave the way she had. Was it marital problems? The pain of knee surgery? Something else? No one seemed to grasp the emotional impact on me of the event I was relating. No one said something like, "God, that must have been so terrifying for you" (or if they did, it felt cursory). No one validated the pain I was exposing as I fought for breath. No one put her hand on mine; no one hugged me. The longer I watched their response in a kind of out-of-body way, the more I felt like a rape victim lying bruised on the floor while everyone rushes to the aid of the attacker. I remember thinking that if I'd been assaulted by a man I'd loved and trusted for fifty-five years who had suddenly turned violent, this wouldn't be an occasion to pick sides; it would be a time full of unconditional sympathy and support.

Later, after we'd all returned home, I asked myself a sickening question: Were we really a women's group or simply a group of women? Just girlfriends? A playgroup masquerading as a support group? I felt sad beyond belief, and startled in the way you might be if you looked in the mirror and saw for the first time wrinkles on your sagging face that you once hoped never to be subjected to.

Not long after that episode I underwent surgery. Again, the response from the Crones felt minimal. *Hope you're doing well,* one e-mailed; *Keep us posted,* another wrote. None of the electronic messages felt like genuine support. They felt instead like courtesy calls, obligatory communication, not taking the time to address trauma in a way that says, "I'm there for you, Sister!"

I recognize that our lives become more complicated as we age. There are adult children coping with life issues; spouses or partners handling health issues; grandchildren who fill our lives; work and other interests. But what had become of our Crone magic? Why did I feel that Croning would never be the same, that it would never be quite so joyful or safe or welcoming? Now our future trips seemed more like respite from life's busy complications. They brought to mind the dots in a quotation that serve to eliminate the complex, nuanced, finer aspects of a statement. They no longer seemed like a time for women to close ranks, to be there—anywhere, anytime—reminding us that we are not alone.

Recently, I had an epiphany about the events of which I write, while reading a simple sentence in Vivian Gornick's compelling book *The Situation and the Story: The Art of Personal Narrative*. Published in 2001, Gornick's little book, so important for writers of creative nonfiction, makes a strong case for authors of effective essays to place themselves in the narrative. To enter not in a narcissistic way, but rather in a way that strengthens their artistic expression about an event. She argues that knowing who is speaking and why, understanding the author's intent, gives larger meaning to an essay.

One sentence in particular compelled me to craft this essay: "[The author] gradually leads us to a deeper insight: the *unwillingness* with which we—all of us—arrive at self-understanding."[4]

Suddenly, there it was, staring me in the face: I had no right to expect my friends or my adopted kids to fill the vast void left by my frequently absent mother. For how could they? The bottomless pit of my longing for her velvet touch, her laughter, her presence—so primal and perpetual—could never be filled now, as it could not be filled during her frequent absences when I was a child, no matter how much attention others paid me. I could not expect others to understand the depth of my wounds (why should they?), or to stanch my bleeding heart.

And whatever it was that pulled my friends, my adopted daughter, the Crones, T., away from my loving them and wanting to return the gift of their presence in my life, well, that was a void created for reasons known only to them which I could no longer strive to fill.

This insight allowed me to come closer to forgiveness in a way that Buddhists believe leads to the end of suffering. It did not, however, lead to total absolution. For surely I have every right to acknowledge the wounds inflicted and the solitude endured by withdrawn friendship, for whatever reasons it occurred, even when the pain it causes is unrecognized and without willful malice. And so, I wrote:

> *In silent grief I lurch forward,*
> *despite the death of trust*
> *In those I trusted wholly to do no harm.*
> *The aching loneliness of solitude*
> *Weighing heavy on this now bruised heart.*

And yet, being now in the center of this narrative, knowing why it is I am compelled to write of events both personal and traumatic, and perhaps having a larger understanding of what transpired, I find greater meaning in reflecting upon these events. The catharsis inherent in sharing personal experience, the very act of telling the story, is both purifying and purposeful.

Vivian Gornick's valuable book taught me this: I am here "only to make the widest and most thoughtful sense of [my] own experience. Out of that alone comes useful extrapolation."[5] Out of it, as well, comes relief, and the self-care that accompanies adult insight, as one strives to forgive not only others, but oneself.

Elayne Clift is a writer, journalist, workshop leader, lecturer, and Vermont Humanities Council Scholar. Formerly an international women's health advocate and educator, she is senior correspondent for the India-based news syndicate Women's Feature Service, *a regular columnist for the* Keene (NH) Sentinel *and the* Commons *(Brattleboro, VT), and a reviewer for the* New York Journal of Books. *Her latest book, with Christine Morton, is* Birth Ambassadors: Doulas and the Re-emergence of Woman-Supported Birth in America *(Praeclarus Press, 2014). She published her first novel,* Hester's Daughters, *a contemporary, feminist retelling of* The Scarlet Letter, *in 2012. She lives in Saxtons River, Vermont, and can be found at www.elayneclift.com.*

Sealed With A Kiss

Elizabeth Searle

My first kiss was a practical joke set up by a pretend friend. Or I call her pretend now, in retrospect. At the time she and her friendship seemed real enough. And the kiss? Lips met, so it counted; in my case, it counted as my number one and only first.

New studies purport to show a hormonal basis for Mean Girls. Back in my day, Mean Girls weren't called the M word. And bullying was likely to be labeled a "practical joke." As if anyone who fell for the joke was simply foolish, impractical.

What on earth is "practical" about a so-called practical joke, hormonally fueled or not? My friend was not pretend, but I'll call her Jen as a pretend name here. It fits. A cool single-syllable name like the trendy seventies name she really sported years ago, in our shared eighth-grade daze in a public school in Kentucky, where, months after she pulled her "prank" on me, Jen herself was publicly punished.

To be honest, I wish that, as my own secret pretend punishment against her, I could name Jen's real name here, in print—or rather, the sullen grudge-holding eighth grader in me wishes I could. I wished it even back when I was still a dreamy, brooding fourteen-year-old, already determined to make my own name as a writer. Someday, I theatrically vowed to myself, I'd write about all of them, the tormented teens who tormented me.

Yet when I had my first nonfiction opportunity to write briefly about my high school woes, in a published anthology titled *Don't You Forget About Me*, I did follow the Simon & Schuster legal staff's advice. I did change the Mean Girl names—except when I gave readings from the essay in question. Then I substituted the real names in order to have my mini-revenge, even if only for a small bookstore crowd.

Can you tell I'm Irish? Never forgive and never forget. Also I am—and surely this made me an irresistible target back in the day—gullible. "Did you know," a real friend asked me when I was old enough to know better, "that *gullible* is not really a word?" "Really?" I asked back earnestly.

For a second, to my friend's eternal bemusement, it seemed plausible to me in this strange unpredictable world that somehow, according to some rules I didn't know, *gullible* was not a word.

By that same hapless logic, I halfway believed—or just wholly *wanted* to believe—my brand-new eighth-grade friend Jen when she started telling me, over and over, "Fred likes you. Fred really really likes you."

(Fred is not his real name either, of course, though it did start with *F*— and you'll see if you read on why that *F* fits.)

So that gives you bit of background before we get to the practical joke itself and its punch line, delivered so lamely yet so memorably by Fred, on behalf of Jen—her way of letting me know I'd been dumped. By her, not Fred.

Fred was just a pawn, a player in this mystifying Mean Girl plan, hatched—one part I know for sure—by Jen herself. Who maybe through some inner hormonal hubbub was "not herself" at that time of her life. From what little I hear, she grew up into a decent person. Are any of us really "ourselves" in the fraught overwrought throes of being fourteen?

Certainly I didn't know who I was back then, especially since I always seemed to be "the new girl." Before our new school in Kentucky, where pretty buxom brunette Jen and her blond sidekick (I'll call her "Dee") seemed so readily to befriend me, I'd been transplanted from a small neighborhood in Pennsylvania, where I had an automatic "best friend" across the street, to a non-neighborhood in rural, red-clay-dirt Greenville, South Carolina.

At the public elementary school there, kids said "Hey" or "Hi." So a gang of Southern-accented belles followed me around saying, as if in friendship, "Hey, Elizabeth. Hey, Elizabeth." After I answered 'Hey' back in my hope-lessly stiff Yankee accent, the girls following me collapsed in fits of derisive giggles, mimicking my lame "Hey" as I scurried away. The next day, as if anew, they'd follow me again, saying, "Hey, Elizabeth. Hey, hey—"

Years later, I can see that maybe those bitchy belles felt my stiff "Hey" was snobby, somehow making fun of *their* accents. Why, I still wonder thirty-plus years later, must teenage girls turn on one another this way?

Why make the lives of fellow teens—trapped together in our acne-marred faces and our tender training-bra'd breasts—even worse? Of course some kids—me, for sure, back then—make it all too easy. We turn timid and passive and mad only on the inside, practically posting a Kick Me sign on our hunched backs.

When my family escaped South Carolina—where for me, at least, Southern hospitality had proved a myth—I vowed that Kentucky would be different. I would be different. And at first, thanks to the surprising friendliness of Jen and Dee, it seemed maybe I was a true "new girl" in more than one way.

I was starting my new life in a brand-new "housing development," grandly named Riverbluff Farms even though there was no bluff, farm or river in sight. The Riverbluff homes seemed to have sprung up all together, freshly painted and nearly identical, the yards more mud than grass. But the mud was rich brown, not red clay, and the grass did seem, to hopeful me, to have a lush bluish tint in our new "Kentucky home."

Still, like the homes of Riverbluff—with hidden leaks beneath the shiny surfaces—things in Kentucky only looked good at first. Our father had taken his new job on impulse. I now know that Dad knew within weeks he had made a big mistake. But he and my mother tried to keep their own tensions and disappointments under the surface. My siblings and I, too, put on game faces heading into our new "new school."

Once again, the accents surrounding us were Southern, sometimes mush-mouthed to our Yankee ears. The right way to say "Louisville," a grinning Jen explained to me on the bus we shared, was to say it slow: "Loo-uh-vull." But she didn't make me repeat it after her; she didn't make fun of my accent or my stop-sign-framed glasses.

Determined not to be mocked at this school, I kept my mouth mostly shut, hiding my braces. I made my smiles brief and close-lipped. So maybe I struck giggling, gregarious Jen as standoffish. Jen and her best pal, Dee, both rode the same bus as me, both more stylish than me in their cool "layered" haircuts and worn jeans with colorful patches on their butts. Plus, Jen even had a boyfriend of sorts, or anyway a sneering jean-jacketed guy who kissed her good-bye one frosty fall afternoon early in the school year.

Jen clamored onto our bus even more giggly than usual and confided in both Dee and me—I happened to be sitting next to Dee—"His teeth felt so cold!"

We all three laughed, together. That afternoon, to my stunned delight, Jen and Dee suggested I hang out with them for a while. They led the way to a half-finished house on the outskirts of Riverbluff Farms, giant plastic sheets shielding the wall-less rooms from the fall chill. I tried to look impassive, cool, when Dee produced a pack of cigarettes. I tried only a dainty puff, scared of coughing, of getting caught.

Jen and Dee laughed that off, but maybe I sealed my doom that day, watching them smoke and gossip in tongue-tied silence. Still, I joined in happily when talk turned to TV and movie stars, those crushes I'd carried with me through our various moves. Robert Redford and David Cassidy for me; Starsky and Hutch for them. I kept to myself my truest crushes on 1940s movie stars and my own secret ambitions to act or to write. I remember being proud of myself for knowing what not to say. For knowing how to seem, or so I hoped—not "too weird" to hang out with those two, Jen and Dee.

We three trooped back to our homes in a companionable huddle against the growing dark and cold. I dared to hope that day that I had made two friends—two more than I'd had in South Carolina.

Jen and Dee began letting me sit with them occasionally in the crowded, confusing cafeteria. I began "helping" Jen with her vocabulary homework. I began "loaning" Jen lunch money, which she never paid back. She could be nice, pretty pudgy-faced dimpled Jen. She sometimes hugged a worshipful boy from the "special" classes. She told me once, offhandedly, that I looked like a girl who was a star thespian at our school, who wore more stylish glasses than mine and excelled like me in English class. Though I was much too shy to approach that girl's always-laughing lunch table, I liked being compared to her. Ultimately, this offhand remark of Jen's triggered me to reach out to the thespian crowd at my next "new school" — where at last, in faraway Arizona, I'd find some real friends.

But first I had to survive eighth grade in Kentucky. We all find our ways to survive. One kid in Kentucky who hung out at both the thespian table and Jen's giggly-girl table was a skinny pale tall boy named Fred. Like me, Fred kept pretty quiet. Unlike me, he shared whole cigarettes with Jen and Dee and shared occasional laughs with the clever sharp-tongued thespian kids.

"Fred likes you; he really likes you," Jen and Dee both started telling me, insistently, as the muddy sunny fall shifted to the blue-gray rainy winter. "Fred likes you; he likes you. You're getting really popular, you know?"

Right—and *gullible* was not really a word. Yet I nodded numbly at Jen when she told me this, despite her stagy smirky smile. Hiding something, I knew deep down. Yet I actually felt a faint dumb stirring of hope. Some game was afoot and I didn't know the rules. But maybe if I played along, I'd win.

Maybe Fred thought that too. Maybe Fred was gay and didn't know it yet. Or maybe he had a crush on Jen and/or Dee. Or maybe he was just a clueless hanger-on, hoping to be accepted any which way, like me. During the "Fred likes you" weeks—and it did go on for weeks—Fred would glance away if I glanced over at him. The day he finalized Jen's pointless prank, he looked—walking between Jen and Dee toward me—like a blank-faced hostage, a prisoner with a jailhouse pallor.

"Fred wants to tell you something," Jen announced to me with her new oversized smile. "He has something really important to tell you." Suddenly, in a gale of giggles, she and Dee disappeared around the cinder-block wall that separated the middle school where we attended eighth grade from the larger cinder-block fortress of the looming high school.

Somehow, in the early-winter Kentucky air, Fred and I were left standing alone in the middle of that in-between walkway, in between classes, facing each other warily. "Fred" spoke my name, my real name.

"Elizabeth," he said stiffly as any bad actor. "I just want to tell you . . ."

He leaned in to me, planted a cold-lipped kiss on my unready un-lip-glossed lips. His lips pressed mine determinedly, as if he were imprinting some seal upon me. *Sealed with a kiss:* the words sprang to my startled mind as Fred pulled back from me. Unblinking, he finished what he wanted to tell me:

"Fuck off."

The *F* word still packed a punch back then. Predictably, that was how this punch line made me feel: punched. As if tall but scrawny Fred had punched me in the stomach. A harsh bell rang.

We were both late. Fred turned like a thief and ran. I followed slowly, the chill Chiclet taste of his lips still on mine. A punch line and punch, yes. But it was—I felt dismally sure as I plodded toward study hall—not really from Fred. It was a message from Jen, my supposed friend. Now ex-friend.

Fuck her, I thought as I slunk into study hall late, unnoticed as always. I slumped in my seat so my long dark hair hid my chilled yet burning face. *At least,* I told myself though it wasn't true, *I saw it coming.*

Fuck her, I'd think to myself often in the coming colder weeks, as Jen and Dee brushed by me in the halls and on the bus, not seeming to see me. The joke was over; our "friendship" was kaput.

Fred himself was suddenly invisible, as if he'd vanished from the school. Or maybe he was just ashamed, just hiding from me the way I started hiding in the herds of blue-jeaned students from all three of them.

So what? I told myself at the time. *It was never real to begin with.* So why did it hurt so much, to be dissed and dumped by a girl who never really had been my friend? A girl who would later become a Special Ed teacher, whose round dimply face forever beams with a sly friendly smile in our high school yearbook.

But Jen's foolish prank—which I'd been foolish enough to more than halfway fall for—left its imprint on me, as if in fact Fred had sealed shut my lips with his clumsy kiss. At any rate, I clammed up at that school, after that kiss. I stayed nearly silent in my solitary lunches and my backseat bus rides. Maybe I could have changed the dynamic if I'd spoken up, faced those girls down. But I spoke up only after raising my hand, only in class.

Later in the school year, Jen got in trouble in English class, building up too many tardies. Our bearded brute of a teacher (I'll call him Mr. C.) used a wood paddle to punish students. The day Jen was to face her "licks," I overheard her nervously announce that she was wearing three pairs of panties under her jeans, that she was sure she would not cry. A point of honor among the cooler tougher "bad girls."

The Roman Colosseum had nothing on a Kentucky classroom on days when kids got licks. Mr. C. solemnly removed from his desk drawer the thick wood paddle—holes drilled into it to make it hurt more. Flushed giggly Jen was led out to the deserted school hall, where a fellow teacher would witness the licks. She braced herself against the lockers and bent over.

The class, including me, sat silent, holding our breaths to hear the resounding *clop clop* as the licks were expertly administered. Usually I would feel pangs of sympathy. Jen rushed into the class ahead of Mr. C. and buried her burningly red face in her arms at her desk, silently crying.

I felt a silent mean satisfaction at that. Some of her new cohorts—she'd dumped Dee too by then—asked if she was okay. A slight sarcastic edge to the question, because she'd lost it and cried. From my desk in the back of the room, I kept my lips sealed shut.

Jen recovered her cool. The licks became a story she told her new bad-girl friends at the new, rowdier lunch table I never went anywhere near. But even back then, in that routinely brutal school, I felt ashamed of myself at how I'd felt secretly satisfied to have Jen punished.

Toward the end of my sojourn in Kentucky, I nabbed a job at a movie theater selling candy, wearing a short-skirted concession-stand dress that oddly flattered my skinny long-legged body. I loved getting to see movies for free. And I loved how the long-haired projectionist and the balding, slightly sleazy theater manager both flirted with me as if I were—in their eyes, at least—a "popular" girl.

I wanted so badly for them to believe I was popular, savvy, and cool like the other candy-stand girls that, when the middle-aged theater manager edged over beside me behind my glass counter and copped a lingering feel of my ass, I stood perfectly still, frozen. Acting like what he was doing was okay. It creeped me out, but I acted like I liked it. Because I wanted him to keep thinking I was a cool girl, a Jen.

Because I wanted that so badly, the first sexual touch I ever experienced from a man, like my first so-called kiss, was all an act. No wonder I fit right in with the misfit melodramatic thespian crowd when, my senior year, in my new "new home" in Arizona, I finally found them. No wonder when I first wrote about the kiss incident years later, I made it into fiction, a short story. The girl in my story gets revenge of a sort on her hapless "Fred."

In the story, she manages to make him the butt of the joke in order to get in good with the Mean Girls who tricked her. A hollow victory for the character in the story. In the story, unlike in my life, I was able to have sympathy for the hapless "Fred" and even for the so-called Mean Girls, nervous too behind their bravado and fake-friend smiles.

I titled the short story "Not Herself," the title referring to a favorite line of mine from my favorite Humphrey Bogart movie, *To Have and Have Not*. 1940s movies were my biggest comfort throughout high school. Their grainy black-and-white universe spoke to my sense of romance as risk, and moral codes as absolutes. Black and white, indeed, to teenage me. Once I joined the theater crowd in Arizona, I found fellow old-movie buffs and fellow hams, all of us almost always "on," always acting.

But at least that thespian crowd was up-front about acting. At least we stuck together and didn't fake the friendships we formed. In a short story by the matchless Alice Munro, a character looks back on melodramatic misbehavior of her youth and wishes they'd all behaved differently. Maybe if I'd found it within my teenage self to speak up and sympathize with Jen over her licks, somehow things might have been different. You never know. Surely it's always best to at least try to act as our best selves. In another Munro story, the narrator mentions in a wise aside that teenage girls are always "playing at" some role, whether it's acting nice or acting mean. Why do we all work so hard at that age to keep our masks and our made-up faces intact, unreadable?

In *To Have and Have Not*, ultracool Bogie is faced with a glamorous woman freaking out, losing her cool in a dangerous situation. He's asked to please forgive her behavior; he's told that this woman is "not herself." And Bogie asks, deadpan, "Oh yeah? Who is she?"

Elizabeth Searle is the author of four books of fiction, most recently Girl Held in Home, *and the librettist of* Tonya & Nancy: The Rock Opera, *a show that has drawn national media attention. Her previous books are the novella* Celebrities in Disgrace, *a finalist for the Paterson Fiction Prize and produced as a short film in 2010; the novel* A Four-Sided Bed, *nominated for an American Library Association book award and currently in development as a feature film; and* My Body to You, *a story collection that won the Iowa Short Fiction Award. Elizabeth's work has been included in nearly a dozen anthologies, including* Knitting Yarns: Writers on Knitting *(W. W. Norton, 2013). Her fiction has appeared in over thirty magazines, including* Ploughshares *and* Redbook. *Elizabeth's theater works have been featured in stories on Good Morning America, CBS, CNN, NPR, the AP, and more. She teaches fiction and scriptwriting at Stonecoast MFA.*

Part Two:
It's Not Always About You

Against the impossible.
Author as bystander,
holding the unfortunate mirror.

Keeping Secrets

Carol A. Cassara

Some one hundred years after it ended, the Civil War hung like a miasma over our small North Florida town. Native Southerners were still suspicious of us "Yankees" back in the 1970s, and so we Northerners tended to band together. Maybe that was how my friendship with Marianne started: two Yanks in a town of Rebels. Maybe. It was a long time ago, and memory fails.

As if being from the North wasn't different enough, Marianne was an activist whose life's work was saving monkeys from research labs. I worked in corporate public relations and volunteered for the same local humanitarian organization in my spare time. Yankees and Damn Yankees, for sure. Other than being born above the Mason-Dixon Line, however, it didn't look like we had much in common except our interest in saving monkeys.

Central casting couldn't have found a better activist than Marianne. Her priorities were clear, even in how she looked, her face bare of makeup and her hairstyle definitely wash-and-wear. Me? I was expert with brushes and powders, straightening my curly hair every day, rolling the top part in a huge roller and bobby-pinning the rest around my head for a straight finish. Jeans and a wrinkled T-shirt were her hallmark; I favored business suits with bows at the neck. Marianne was married with two small girls she brought to every save-the-monkeys meeting; I was married, but childless.

Marianne was an introvert who played her personal life close to the vest; I wore my life on my chest.

But we developed a bond over what was far less obvious: I carried the long-hidden shame of my father's verbal and physical abuse, and Marianne was the first friend I'd told about this deeply rooted ache, and that my mother, also a victim, had been too afraid to step in. Maybe that confidence opened the door to hers. Slowly, awkwardly at first, she confided her deepest insecurities and the most painful, intimate parts of her childhood. I was surprised and touched: I knew trust didn't come easily to her. Over time, she talked haltingly about her grandmother's suicide. Her mother's insecurities. And her own. Over eight years of friendship, those deep talks cemented our bond, and since we connected on the most important levels, neither of us cared that we weren't alike in other ways.

We did both chain-smoke, though, back in that day. The ashtray in her small, beat-up Volvo overflowed, leaving barely any room for me to stub out my own butts. We spent a lot of time in that Volvo, going from meeting to meeting, talking.

On those rides, Marianne had good advice for me about everything—my messed-up family, work, life. She was smart and passionate, if a little doctrinaire about animal research. I liked being around her and I liked that she liked me, which was important because ours was the deepest friendship I'd made since high school.

"One day you're going to be really mad at your mother," she said.

"What do you mean? Mom was a victim too!" I protested.

"Trust me," she said. "There will come a day when you will be angry at your mom for not stepping in."

No way, I thought.

Marianne's permanent brow furrow—she was just thirty-one—made me worry that she was overcommitted. A full-time job and her work advocating for animals filled every waking hour. She smoked, she drove, she plotted. It appeared to me there was hardly time for her to be a mom, or for her daughters to be children; they were serious and quiet, more like mini adults. I noticed Marianne didn't spend much time on her marriage, either. Her husband, Evan, a bank president, was busy with his career, so Marianne had the girls all the time, even at meetings that sometimes lasted late into the night. Amy and Lisa would sit quietly, bent over homework or coloring books, while a small group of activists postured and planned. Marianne was pleased when her girls began spouting the same rhetoric we'd hear at meetings, but I always thought she brought them along mostly out of guilt: if she'd left them with a sitter, she'd never see them.

I saw so much of them that they felt like my nieces and they treated me like a favored aunt. The two were sweet, but different from other children I knew: guarded, like their mother; trust had to be earned. Even at ages five and eight, I could see them size up situations before responding. I figured they learned this from their mother. That's what kids do, right?

Evan? Handsome and charming. But Evan fucked around. Boldly, too: it wasn't unusual to see him out and about hand in hand with a smartly put-together young woman who looked the antithesis of his wife. Everyone in town knew, including me. No one said a word, including me. How do you tell your best friend her husband's cheating? It felt taboo. I was a young thirty, naive, inexperienced in these things. I had no idea how to broach the subject. Anyway, what good would it do? But it nagged at me whenever I'd see him.

Marianne was not unattractive, but she did nothing to enhance what God gave her. In one of those rare moments when she let her guard down, she told me she had never felt pretty. It didn't help that her husband was out on the town every night, I thought. What wife in that situation wouldn't have low self-esteem?

Once, she hinted that she knew Evan saw other women.

"I know he's flirtatious," she told me, "and it bothers me." She didn't make eye contact.

"Why do you stay with him?" I asked, careful not to mention cheating outright.

"Men as handsome as Evan have never been interested in me," she said. "I could never find anyone else as handsome. No, this is it, for me."

I thought that was outmoded thinking for 1980 and told her so. Men in the animal-advocacy orbit liked her and respected her commitment, and I thought one even had a crush on her. John might not have been as handsome as Evan, but he was nice-looking, with a sweet nature and a good heart. When I told her I thought the shaky pretext for John's calls and the way he looked at her signaled an interest beyond protest logistics, she just laughed and shook her head in disbelief.

Life went on and so did our friendship. We grew as close as sisters; at least it seemed that way to me. After a decade of friendship, I spoke easily of the things that troubled me. My difficult relationship with my sister. My mother's meddling in my marriage. Marianne continued to let her defenses down with me a little at a time. What else might lie under her veil of reserve? I'd wonder, knowing she'd let me in at her own pace or not at all.

I continued my involvement with the monkey group mostly because

Marianne's time was at such a premium and it was the only way to be sure I'd see her regularly. Our friendship was conducted in the car on the way to or from events, or at dinners at her house. She cooked a sit-down dinner with meat, two sides, and dessert for Evan and their girls every night, and I ate with them about once a week when my husband had class. Despite Evan's failings, he was likable: cordial, funny, personable.

And then my husband left me. I was unprepared, and I was a mess. Life seemed gray with no future. I wanted to curl up in a ball in the backseat of my Oldsmobile and never move. I considered suicide, but Marianne walked me through my grief without being intrusive, always available. She invited me to dinner every night and let me haunt her house like a crazy relative who lived in the attic. She took me to meetings, listened to my pity party, dried my tears. We grew even closer.

I wonder now if my heartbreak back then looked like a scary cautionary tale, something that might happen to her if she ever gave Evan an ultimatum. But at the time, I had no thought for her motivations or worries; this was *my* pity party and mine alone.

After a while, I recovered and began seeing a man who wanted to marry me as soon as possible. Though she never said so directly, I knew Marianne didn't like Duane, thought he wasn't right for me. She was right: it had all the hallmarks of a rebound relationship that wouldn't go the distance. But I was in love, and I married him less than a year after my husband left. Marianne was my maid of honor.

"You look pretty," I said, smiling, when I saw her standing awkwardly in a cocktail dress and a bit of makeup. Embarrassed, she grinned and shook it off. "I feel like I'm playing dress-up."

About six months into my new marriage, Marianne stopped returning my calls. Suddenly, without any provocation I could identify, she was unavailable. Gone. As if she no longer existed. Dead to me.

I cornered her at a meeting. I begged her to tell me what was wrong. "It's not you," she said.

"Then what is it? Is it Duane?"

"No. It isn't you." She looked away. That's all she would say. I kept at her. She stonewalled me. It was inconceivable, but true: I'd been dumped by my closest friend, the woman who was dearer than a sister. She had erased herself from my life. And worse: with no explanation.

My brain spun, seeking a reason. Was it this episode or that? Was it really Duane? What had I done? Nothing made sense except that she probably didn't like my new husband and didn't want to be around him. She'd told me that wasn't true, but I didn't believe her.

For almost ten years, my two closest confidantes had been my first husband and Marianne, and now they'd both abandoned me without explanation. Why? What sin was so grievous that it could cause my best friend to walk out of my life like she had, knowing how hurt I'd be?

What about Amy and Lisa, who had been an almost daily part of my life? I missed helping them with homework. Coloring Easter eggs. Trick-or-treating. I missed standing at the stove next to Marianne while she cooked, talking over the sound of the vent fan. And I missed the long talks in her car about life and love and psychology, cigarette smoke blowing out the windows.

Three years passed. We were cordial at the few meetings I still attended, but otherwise interacted like strangers—which is to say, not at all. My new marriage wasn't going well, and I finally left it and my city, now a city of loss, moving far away from all of everything. I made sure Marianne had my new address and phone number, but I didn't try to stay in touch beyond two casual letters. She didn't respond.

I established a new life, a new career, and new friends in my new city. I did not join the local animal rights group.

A few more years passed before I returned to the area for a visit with other friends. Driving my rental car down the boulevard that led to Marianne and Evan's small red brick house, I could only think about how many times in the past I'd made the same drive.

That night I called her. Surprised, she invited me for dinner. It was an unexpected gesture, just like old times, and I was thrilled. The girls, now in their teens, seemed happy to see me, but quickly disappeared to their rooms to do homework. Marianne and I made clumsy conversation in the kitchen for a while, about nothing, really. While she fixed dinner, I wandered down the hall to the family room to say hello to Evan, who was watching a football game. We chatted for a few minutes and then, apropos of nothing, he mentioned that he was in therapy.

"Really?" I said, thinking back to his blatant infidelities. "For what?" I was sure he'd say "marital issues."

He hesitated and then blurted, "For inappropriate contact with the girls."
I stared in disbelief. My knees went weak. I couldn't breathe or speak.
I wanted to hit him. *Oh my God, those poor girls,* I thought. Then I won-
dered, why would he tell *me*? What was the purpose?

Evan's voice interrupted my thoughts. "It happened a few years ago." He
referenced a job he'd had at the time.

And then I knew. The time Evan described correlated with the time
Marianne froze me out. Exactly.

It all added up. The way the little girls had seemed cautious and distrust-
ing. Marianne's overnight withdrawal from my life. Her stonewalling of my
attempts to get to the bottom of her distant behavior.

Still, why hadn't Marianne told me? Why hadn't she let me support her as
she'd once done for me? Why hadn't she trusted our friendship enough to know
I'd be there for her? Perhaps, instead of offering comfort and safety, our intimate friendship had threatened her ability to keep the biggest secret of her life.
Marianne had dumped me not because she didn't need or trust me, but because
she wanted to ensure I wouldn't find out. So I wouldn't judge her for staying
with a man who had committed the greatest sin a father could commit.

And she wasn't completely wrong. I would have judged. He had abused
their girls and she had let him back into the house. She must have known I'd
question that decision aggressively. My stomach churned when I thought
of what Amy and Lisa had been through.

Marianne should have protected her daughters. Her words so many
years ago echoed in my head: *One day you're going to be really mad at your
mother.* Had she really been talking about her own fear? Had she already
known what lay ahead for her?

Evan's revelation was stunning. My mind could not fathom the act or his
ability to do it. I was struck mute.

Just then, Marianne called us to dinner. She was at the sink draining rice.
"He told me," I whispered.

She didn't look up. I didn't say anything more, and looking back, I regret
it. But what does one say after learning something like that? Should I have
walked out? Demanded to know why she let him live with the girls? Made
a scene? My brain raced with unasked questions, and because I didn't
know what to say or do, I didn't do anything.

After an uncomfortable dinner, I made my excuses and left as soon as I
could.

I thought about how their father's actions had likely changed the girls' lives forever. About how awful it must be to be so insecure you'd stay with a husband who had been "inappropriate" with your daughters. I wondered who had been responsible for that original deep wound to Marianne's self-esteem. Had it been Evan, back in their high school days? Had it deepened with every infidelity? I wondered if Marianne still had sex with him.

And finally, I thought about how it had felt to be dumped by Marianne without explanation. How I had blamed myself, my then husband; how I had tortured myself needlessly trying to figure out what I had done, when in fact she'd told me the truth: It wasn't me. It wasn't Duane. She just hadn't told me the *whole* truth.

As I drove back to my hotel, I considered how some things are just inconceivable.

Two decades later, my first husband and I reconciled. Compiling a guest list for our wedding reception, we talked about the friends we'd known in our first marriage. He mentioned Marianne and Evan.

"They were a big part of your life back then," he said. "It would be fun to tell them we're back together and to see them again."

I told him the story. His eyes widened. He was quiet for a moment. Then said he would be extremely uncomfortable if Evan attended. His jaw set. "I'm fine with inviting her. Alone. But she's your friend. You decide."

I thought about it for days. Marianne had been there when he'd left, and I hoped she'd rejoice with me at our reconciliation. I couldn't figure out how to invite her but not her husband. In the end I addressed an invitation to both, and put it in the mail.

They didn't respond.

At the reception I half expected them to turn up anyway, in the kind of surprise an old friend might plan. But no.

It had been almost three decades since those confidences in the smoky Volvo, and, I imagined, much trauma.

There was never another word from Marianne.

I'd like to say that I never thought about them again. But that wasn't true. Our friendship was part of my history, a time in my young adulthood when I was just learning about life. When having a best friend to share my most intimate confidences with had been a new experience.

Once in a while, on a sleepless night, I'll think of Marianne and her girls.

The girls are probably married with older children of their own now. Had things been different, they'd still be my favored "nieces." I picture them as children sitting at a monkey-advocacy meeting, intent on homework, their dark hair falling over their shoulders. And I send up a silent blessing that their lives and those of their own children be whole and happy.

Sometimes, that's all you can do. And sometimes, it just has to be enough.

Carol A. Cassara is a writer, blogger, and sometime college instructor who is busy living life out loud in the San Francisco Bay area and wherever else in the world her frequent travels take her. She has been a contributor to the Chicken Soup for the Soul *anthologies, among others. She shares her life with her crazy dog and very patient husband.*

All Talk and Trousers

Carrie Kabak

When Bethan first met Bob Rafferty, when I brought him back to our digs in Monthermer Road, she considered him quite the catch. "Oh my God," she said in the kitchen. "Hang on to this one, *cariad*. How much sugar does he take in his coffee?"

She filled a mug with boiling water and instant granules, and I didn't have the heart to tell her he preferred Colombian. That he had a penchant for a full-bodied roast. That he had a palate for a vibrant, complex, and more classically balanced brew. That he might toss his curls as he laughed and tut-tutted at the Nescafé instant, despite it being Blend 37.

"Add a spoon of demerara," I told Bethan.

Pickle it with sugar so he won't notice.

"His voice is *amazing*," she breathed.

To my friend's ears, Rafe's Derry accent was fascinating. Captivating. Musical. Raised within an Irish community, I didn't see it that way, and was scolded for being indifferent. According to Bethan, I was the luckiest devil alive.

"What's he doing in Cardiff?" she wanted to know.

"Looking for work."

Bethan's eyes twinkled. "He's so *mature*," she said. "So *sexy*."

"He dreams of being a head chef."

"So *motivated*," she added.

Rafe was forty-one years old back then. Going gray at the gills. Divorced twice. A whole seventeen years older than me. Craggily handsome and witty and smart. Charismatic and seemingly credible.

I met him in a fish and chip shop in Cathays, where I worked while I was a student and where he became a late-night regular.

And now, four teaching years later, as Bethan and I sit in the staff room at Eglwys Newydd Primary School, "Rafe certainly has the gift of the gab," I tell her.

But she doesn't understand.

"He's all talk and trousers," I explain.

She shrugs her shoulders. She sees him as enigmatic and downright intriguing. She sees him going places one day.

"Nothing much has happened so far, Bethan."

"He's a highly creative cook," she says. "You can't deny that."

"I can't sleep," I say. "I haven't had a full night's sleep for weeks and I feel like pure shite."

I search for compassion in Bethan's eyes. Wait for comforting words. A touch of the hand. Some sympathy before we return to board and chalk and disruptive eight-year-olds. While we have the room to ourselves.

"As soon as my head hits the pillow, I'm off rehashing fragments of conversation, searching for answers, wondering where life with Rafe is going," I say. "If anywhere at all."

Bethan resumes her knitting, only half listening to me. Silently mouthing instructions. Slip one. Purl one. Pass slipped stitch over.

She has become distant of late. Not as eager to go shopping with me. Or share a drink. Or see a film. These days, she rarely spends longer than ten minutes on the phone.

"No wedding bells, then," she finally says.

With Rafe, any talk of commitment is woolly and matted, like a lump of old felt. There's never been any definite conclusion.

I shake my head. "It's been almost a month since I last saw him, Bethan." And he hasn't bothered to find out why.

"He takes me for granted," I explain. "Like I'll always be there."

Bethan rolls up her knitting. Tightly. Precisely. Packs it with her skeins of blue and beige yarn. "Go on," she says.

Rolling her eyes.

Sighing.

Have I done something wrong? Hurt her in any way? Insulted her? Is she mad at me?

I reel out my story in hopes of restoring our friendship. I relate personal details, determined to rebuild the unique bond we once shared. I reenact scenes to paint the total picture.

Rafe postpones, delays, and keeps putting off, I tell her. He leaves everything until the last second. He drags his feet, he dawdles, he reschedules, and he has been unemployed since I first met him. He plays back phone messages not caring what I hear, because we're a team, pet, which means there shouldn't be any secrets between us, should there? Debt collectors have important matters to discuss, Mr. Rafferty, please contact them immediately. Mortgage, hire purchase, electric, gas, and water. He'll get his act together soon, my little love, my only darling, come on, have *some* faith. Of course we'll get married! As soon as things straighten out, pet, that's when. Don't look at him like that! Honest to God, he's trying, so quit with the nagging and constant bloody *whining*. Jesus Christ almighty.

"Rafe allows every opportunity to fizzle away, Bethan."

One business idea after another suffers a lingering death, while I keep him afloat.

"Then leave him," says Bethan.

Her voice is like the clip of the scissors.

"And be done with it."

She rap-taps the table with her fingernails.

Studies a corner of the ceiling.

Eventually tips her head in my direction and asks if there's more.

Arched eyebrows. Her mouth a sharp line.

Bethan's aloofness and what verges on hostility began exactly three weeks ago. I know, because I've been counting the days. So far, I've shied away from acknowledging I've been dumped as a friend. Her once best friend forever. Every niggling question has remained inside my head because I don't want to hear answers that would only confirm my worst fears.

Carping on about Rafe has driven her insane.

My talking of nothing else.

I've become a windbag. A pathetic bore.

And there's only one thing left to do now.

Try to rescue something I can't bear losing.

Bethan's new skirt, in pink georgette, flutters at her knees as she makes for the door. Her hems are shorter. Her black hair longer than it was at college. Her eye shadow heavier, her foundation thicker, her perfume more musky and spiced.

I round the corner and accelerate into Claude Road. Rafe lives in the third house along, the one that hunkers down behind an ivy-infested motte.

He likes ivy, because you don't have to mow it.

Splats of rain hit me sideways as I step into the atmosphere of a steam bath. The sky is mauve and there's a smell of dirt, seawater, and tarmac. A familiar blend that usually predicts the onslaught of a storm.

When Rafe opens his porch door, "Where have you been?" he says. "Here, let me help you with that old bag. Jesus, what do you have in here? Homework?"

I mark thirty exercise books every weekend. Nothing has changed.

He pads toward me in leather moccasins. No socks. Showing a bare ankle is cool these days, pet. Wearing a threadbare sweater. Sporting a black beret pulled down over one ear.

"Are you feeling sick, love?" He peers over his bifocals. Half-moons. Wire-rimmed. Held together with a spot of glue.

"I haven't slept all week," I say.

He thinks I look awful pale. That I could do with some color in my cheeks. And when the rain falls as a blanket, he says we'd better run inside.

He smothers my face with kisses, and his face is unshaved, feeling like sandpaper, as it always does, and his breath is laced with garlic. Then his lips press over mine, and they insist I respond, but I push him away, which makes him ask, "What's the matter, pet?"

"Same old story," I say.

He rubs at the furrows in his forehead. "Let's have a nice evening together, love. I haven't seen you in a month. Where in God's name were you?"

"You didn't care where I was, Rafe."

"Sure, I didn't want to go troubling a busy woman like you."

Tears glass my eyes, but he chooses not to acknowledge that. My crying makes him weary, as does my obsession with the past and my long lists that itemize his faults and his failures. I plague him with accusations. I grill and quiz and question him. My scenes exhaust him. The drama drains him. He's devastated when I doubt his love. Let's move on, he always says. We're soul mates, pet. Peas in a pod. We're meant for each other. Sure, wasn't that always God's plan?

And now he takes my hand. "Will you stay tonight?" he whispers, his mouth brushing my ear. "Will you sleep in my bed?" His smile is slow, his expression suggestive. Not waiting for an answer, he walks his fingers up my arm and asks if I've eaten yet, and when I tell him I'm not hungry, he still says he'll make us an omelet.

"Let's go to the kitchen, pet."

I lean against the tiles Rafe hasn't gotten around to grouting yet. Tiles with little plastic crosses filling the gaps. His cookbooks are piled on the microwave and crammed onto shelves. They run along the baseboards. They lean against the fridge. His collection is huge, all of them acquired or borrowed or taken as gifts. He is indulged, pampered, and spoiled by sisters, ex-lovers, and friends because of his irresistible appeal and magnetic charm.

He passes me butter, eggs, chives, and a block of cheese. Ingredients he couldn't have bought without help.

"Put them on the counter, pet," he says.

And then he examines my face. Searches for clues. Watches the flick of my eyes, listens to the timing of my breath. He's checking the climate before he starts talking. Talking is one thing Rafe is good at. He'll overwhelm you with his words and reasoning and opinions. You'll find yourself hanging on to every syllable, nodding in agreement, regardless of your original conviction or outlook. You'll stay propped against his kitchen wall listening and watching as he flambés and sautés and blends. You'll listen for hours, totally rapt. Everyone does.

"There's a little restaurant for sale in Splott," he says.

"That's an iffy area, Rafe."

"Struggles are part of its history, pet."

Splott is colorful.

Eclectic.

Filled with community spirit.

"Just wait till you see the place," he says. "Wait till you hear what's included in the price!"

There's a six-burner range with fryers, he says, and steamers, a salamander, and three sinks. Fridges and freezers. Reach-ins and walk-ins. Tables, chairs, banquettes, and a bar.

And when he cracks the eggs for the omelets, his smile widens. "We could really make it happen this time, pet."

"We can't buy a restaurant," I say.

He slivers cheddar painstakingly.

Chops chives minutely.

"Rafe?"

Keeping his head down, he squeezes a dishrag and then wipes the Formica that borders the stovetop, paying special attention to the seams and the grooves. Going over twice.

"How about we dip into your savings for the capital, pet?" he says.

A steady thud fills my ears. How much money have I already lavished on this man, to rescue him, tide him over, or keep the roof over his head?

"Sweetheart?" He turns to face me. "What do you think?"

His voice is an undulating hum as he sweet-talks and reasons and wheedles. As he pinches my chin, strokes my cheek, and touches the tip of my nose. "Come on, pet," he says. "Think about it. It's very simple. We could live together, here, in my place."

We're safe for two weeks, love, he says, before his house goes into foreclosure, but best we settle matters ASAP, yeah? His place would be easier to manage, he says. Less expensive to maintain. All he needs from me is, hold on, he has the info in his pocket. Ah. Here we go.

He spreads a letter onto the draining board and smoothes out the creases. He fishes for a pen in the cutlery drawer before circling the amount required to reinstate his loan. And in the process, he delivers the final blow to my heart.

I press my fists against my eyes to ease a searing pain. All I see are blotches, specks, and gliding streaks of color. "Do you think I'm a dimwit?"

I fold my arms tight and back into the corner of the kitchen so he can't touch me. "*Do* you?"

But he doesn't answer. He whisks the eggs instead.

"*Do you?*" I yell.

"For Christ's sake!" he says. "Shut the hell up, or you'll have the neighbors calling the bloody police."

Then he melts butter in the pan, and he won't turn around, and I'm reduced to wringing my hands and walking in circles. What made me think he'd ever change?

I call him a scheming bastard. A con artist.

An . . . *exploiter*.

And he's barely audible when he claims he can't believe what I'm saying.

I look up at the sagging drywall and weep, not wanting to meet his gaze. It feels like something has died, and I'm left reeling, the grief profound, because there's only one route to take now, no matter how hard the wrench.

When he tries to hold me, clamp me tight, I pummel his chest.

"Quit hitting me!" he roars, and his rage is the trigger that sends me galloping to the living room.

His living room. His domain. I look at the cushions ripped by cat claws, and at the rugs that are scrambled with pattern and drab with stains. I look at cupboards that spew papers, brochures, and discarded plans. At drawers that bulge with unopened bills, collections, and cutoff dates, and I wonder what made me think I could tackle all this. What made me believe I could manage and mend? Whatever drove me to take Rafe on in the first place?

There's a splintering crash of plates. "Fuck," he says. *"Fuck."*

Something new catches my eye. A throw on the sofa, hand-knitted in a chaotic array of stripes. A piece of work Bethan held up to show the staff at Eglwys Newydd only three weeks ago.

Only three weeks ago.

At Southerndown Beach, I step over jellyfish, rotting rope, and bits of plastic, all twisted together along a line of silt and other washed-up debris. I keep on walking, my sandals sinking, until I reach the water.

The waves crash, lightning rips through the sky, and the wind cuts to my bones as I analyze what could have happened. Did I just foil some sort of plot?

Were Bethan and Rafe in this together?

But she told me to leave him.

Was he messing with us both?

I vow to leave Cardiff and start a new life, so I'll never know.

And by the time I reach my apartment, when the rain is reduced to a mere drumbeat—

I feel as free as a bird.

Carrie Kabak is author of Cover the Butter *(Penguin Putnam), an Independent Booksellers Pick. Her essays appear in* For Keeps *and* He Said What? *(Seal Press),* Exit Laughing *(North Atlantic Books), and* Faith *(Simon & Schuster). Her second novel,* Deviled Egg, *is in progress. Carrie is a creative technician at Hallmark Cards Inc. and a designer for Pan Macmillan and other major publishers. Born and raised in the UK, she now lives in Missouri with her husband, a professional cook. They share five sons, two Labradors, two cats, and two birds.*

Foundation

Rachel Ambrose

Elle had been acting strangely, I knew that much. Her open, easy laughter had changed key just slightly. But I found her beautiful anyway, so it never occurred to me to say anything until it was too late.

She and I had been friends since freshman year of college, and now we found ourselves in the fall of our junior year. In contrast to the little white gloves our small, conservative school encouraged us to wear, Elle flaunted short, deep red hair (often dyed redder) and an arresting pair of green eyes, greener than I could ever imagine. Her skin was dotted with freckles. She was curious, practiced misandry with abandon, and yet she loved makeup and perfume. She desperately wanted to be a lesbian, "but I like cock too much, Rach," she often told me with a pout of regret. Gloria Steinem was her personal hero. I may have been a little bit in love with her. Southern girls are made of contradictions beneath their long, curved eyelashes. With her signature mix of debutante and punk, she had a soft North Carolina coastal drawl and listened to bands I'd never heard of, like Blue October and Phish.

I thought we were doing well that autumn. I had been to her family's house in Wilmington. Our parents had met and gotten along famously. I was even friends with her sisters on Facebook. We had had a rousing sophomore year, full of boys, drama, and penne alla vodka at our favorite Italian restaurant. "Mmm, Rach, let's get something delicious!" she would say as she showed up at my door around dinnertime, her tongue darting across her soft lips, as she bobbed up and down on the balls of her black Converse-encased feet. It was an irresistible invitation, and I agreed every time, whether I had the money or not. A moment of awkwardness would always come as the check arrived. Paying for a fifteen-dollar meal twice a week ate away at the hundred dollars a month my parents gave me. With her family's big house and her father's medical practice, I knew Elle had money to burn, and sometimes I would look up hopefully, making the reach for my wallet slower than it had to be, in case she was feeling generous. Sometimes I would get lucky and she would pay. I could pretend it was a date, then.

Elle was living off campus, sharing an apartment with two other girls, and I would come over every so often to smoke weed and eat chocolate ice cream. During one of my visits, once we had gotten stoned and were sprawled out on her carpet, she said, "Wanna go to Belk tomorrow and get our makeup done? Our bodies are temples, you know, and it's our job to decorate them. Eye shadow is, after all, God's apology to women for creating the patriarchy!"

I cringed inwardly. The year before, I had had a brief fling with Clinique foundation and concealer. It had gotten to the point where I felt I couldn't leave my dorm room without putting some on, and my mother had given me a look when she'd seen me. "That just doesn't look natural on you," she'd said. I stopped wearing the makeup soon after. Now, lying there on the carpet, I twirled a chunk of hair around my finger and ran it across my lips to steady my nerves. "I dunno, Elle," I said. "I just don't want to get all OCD with it again, you know? Isn't having a healthy mind-set about yourself more important than looking fierce?"

She narrowed her eyes at me. "I've never had that issue, the whole OCD thing. I don't know why you do."

"Well, excuse me if I don't understand exactly how my messed-up brain works," I said, continuing to twirl my hair. Elle watched me, her eyes still narrowed.

"You know," she said. "Makeup would really help you with your tics. If we cut your hair super short, you'd stop playing with it, and if we put some nice moisturizer and BB cream on your face, you'd probably stop picking at your skin. People have been talking to me about that, FYI, like, how gross it is and why do I hang out with you. It's just so unfair to me, Rach."

I winced. My tics were anxiety-driven: I twirled my hair or picked at my face when I was bored or nervous, or when I needed my brain to slow down. It had never occurred to me that other people might be bothered by them, or that they might be affecting me socially. "Well, I'm sorry for the awkwardness," I responded huffily. "But they calm my brain down, and everyone else can just deal with them. If you were a real friend, you'd tell them that."

"Sounds like somebody needs therapy," she said.

"Sure," I said, laughing. "I get a hundred bucks a month, Elle. That's enough for, what, one therapy session? Yeah, that would be so helpful." I rolled my eyes.

"I paid for your dinner the other night!" she replied, as if for the cost of one fifteen-dollar dinner, Sigmund Freud himself might come on down from heaven and perch on the couch. "God, you can be such a mooch sometimes."

I didn't say anything else after that. If she wanted to be a martyr, she could carry that cross on her own. After a while, I got up from the floor and walked out, wending my way back to campus.

A few days later, I came back from classes to find a note pushed under my door. I hadn't seen Elle since the day we got stoned together, and it surprised me to see her curlicue handwriting on the notebook page. The note said, simply and devastatingly, *I can't be friends with you anymore. I'm sorry, there's just too much pressure. Be well.*

I stared at the note. What had happened to her? When had she ever buckled to "pressure?" What did that even mean?

I cried alone in my mess of a room, littered with leftover Chinese takeout containers, notebooks, and the feel of something newly dead. I sat there, heartbroken, faced for the first time with the notion that all my private insecurities about myself as a woman, all those worries that I was too weird, too strange, not good enough, were true.

I took a very long shower and scrubbed at my skin with my loofah, hard, using every last ounce of soap. I dragged out my Clinique and made up my face. I considered chopping off all my hair. But then something kicked in, stubbornness, a strength. I stopped in the middle of looking for the scissors and I thought, *Wait one minute. I'm not even dating this girl! It's her problem, not mine.* I stomped around my dorm room in a moment of righteous anger, willing her to hear my raging footfalls from miles away. But I couldn't bring myself to fight with her about it. She was too right, *and* too wrong. I've always been horrible with confrontation, so I just never spoke to her again. She disappeared out of my life like a vanished raindrop on a summer sidewalk. I found other friends who liked me without trying to change me. The difference between us, it was not a bridgeable distance, this is clear to me now. She used foundation to cover up her flaws. But I came to our friendship with my flaws and my foundation firmly in place and, under my feet, an invisible liquid cloud that supported me better than any flimsy cream or powder ever could.

Rachel Ambrose is a queer writer who enjoys cooking eggs for dinner and committing random acts of feminism. Her work has been previously published in 2014: A Year in Stories, The Colton Review, CutBank Literary Magazine, *and* Crack the Spine. *She sometimes tweets @victorywhiskey.*

The Professional Critic

Diane Spodarek

She would call and read one of her poems over the telephone: the first draft, the second draft, the third, and the final. When she was satisfied with it, she would slip the poem into a plastic sleeve and put it in a three-hole binder, where it rested with the others. The binder sat in a bookcase, on a shelf with how-to books: how to love, how to cure, how to cook, how to paint with numbers. She said she wanted to hear one of my poems but she would have to call me back. She had to move her car.

She called to ask for my recipe for vegetarian chili. Is it three beans or four? Three or four, either way.

With a heavy sigh she said, "It has to be perfect for my party Saturday night."

"Fantastic," I said. "I hope I can get a babysitter."

After a long pause she said, "I thought I already told you. The party is only for important people: professional artists and dealers, and critics like myself." After another pause, she filled the silence with a proposal: "Do you want to be my bartender? I can't pay you and you can't talk to anyone. You have to be professional."

She called to tell me that she slept with the poet I was seeing, the one from California who was in town for the poetry slam, the same poet I sipped endless cups of chamomile tea with while discussing Ginsberg and Sexton. She said she was sure I wouldn't mind; he was more her type than mine. He likes Proust, she said, and so do I. He was very sweet, she said; he was hesitant because of you, but I assured him it was okay. I'm only telling you because he hasn't called. Have you heard from him?

She sat across from me at my kitchen table and read the letter she'd written to her son. With each sentence that began with *I*, her words rose from the page, wrapped around her throat, and choked her. After reading "Love, Mother," she smiled with the expectant look of someone who was about to take a bow. "I'm not the emotional type," she said, "but he was only two when I left." A westerly wind blew through the kitchen window. The slats in the metal blinds applauded her performance, but her face morphed from delight to the realization she had revealed too much. I flinched when she came toward me, but I had nothing to fear. Instead of a perfunctory hug, she adjusted her fanny pack and held out her hand as if to a stranger. I offered my hand in return. She shook it with a professional one-two shake and left.

Diane Spodarek is a Canadian-American artist and writer, a recipient of artists' fellowships from the NEA, the New York Foundation for the Arts, and the Michigan Council for Arts and Cultural Affairs. She has been published in KGB Bar Lit Magazine *and anthologized widely, including in* Young Women's Monologues from Contemporary Plays, Tribes 12, Reverie: Ultra Short Memoirs, *and the* Nuyorican's Estrellas en el Fuego *(Stars in the Fire) anthology. Her video art is archived in the New Museum's XFR STN project collection. She lives in NYC's Westbeth Artists' Housing. Find her at www.westbeth.org/wordpress/artist/diane-spodarek-writer-artist-performer and www.dangerousdiane.blogspot.com.*

Boring Baby

Louise Krug

The text said, *First I have to go see this boring baby.*

The baby was mine.

Jam sent the text to me by accident. It was supposed to go to another friend of hers. A friend who, like her, did not have a baby. A law student who lived downtown. A babe. Jam, the kind of woman whose exes never got over her, was going to have fun with her after the chore of seeing us: me and my baby.

Jam called two seconds after I read the text and said, "Did you just read that?"

"Yes," I said.

"I'll be right there."

When she came to the door, we went into my daughter's room without talking first. My daughter was four months old and, admittedly, not doing much. She lay on her back in the crib and waved her hands in the air. Blew spit bubbles. Pooped.

"Are you mad?" Jam asked as I changed a diaper.

I nodded my head. I hadn't spoken yet.

"You know I didn't mean it, right?" she said. "It was a joke."

I nodded again, picked my daughter up off the changing table.

Of course the rest of her visit was terrible. We laid my daughter on a blanket, sat on the floor, and watched her. Jam left after fifteen minutes. I never saw her again. We e-mailed a couple of times—a dance of apologies, acceptance, and attempts at forgiveness—but it wasn't enough. A few months after the text we stopped writing.

I didn't know how to write about it that day and, almost two years later, I still don't. I get the joke of how boring babies are, and I'm sure I made the same sort of jokes not too long before I had my own baby. It's like kidding about married couples if you're single—how lame they are, going out to dinners at Applebee's and renting rom-coms on a Saturday night.

Except it's not like that at all.

I didn't need any reminder that by having a baby I was getting to be a drag, especially not from Jam. Her life was action-packed. She stayed up until dawn writing brilliant stories, spent what was for me an entire paycheck on wine in one trip to the liquor store, and did things like vacation in a yurt in Arkansas. Her mother was from Egypt, her father from Connecticut. Mine were from Kansas. I ate dinner while it was still light out. I drank wine spritzers that came in six-packs. I hugged.

Days before the boring-baby text happened, Jam and I were Skyping, and she told me that my boobs looked huge. "The rest of me is swollen too," I said, trying to laugh. "I know this one woman, and she's skinnier than she was before she had her baby!" I said. I was in a wardrobe of strictly yoga pants and my husband's T-shirts. I couldn't remember when the last time was that I'd tweezed my eyebrows. I communicated with the outside world through the Internet. I was a new mom.

"Well, ask that woman what she does," Jam said. She was trying to be helpful, to help me feel good about myself again. But I was surprised. I needed her to say that I looked great, that I had all the time in the world to get thin, and that I appeared downright lean to her right then, as a matter of fact. But that wasn't what I got.

I read somewhere that our best friends aren't the people who we like the most, but the people who like us the most. What did I like about Jam? What did she like about me? I couldn't remember, but I wished I could. It might have helped.

Louise Krug is the author of the memoir Louise: Amended *(Black Balloon Publishing, 2012), which was named one of the Top 20 Best Nonfiction Books of 2012 by* Publishers Weekly. *Recently, she has had essays and stories in* Parcel, Paragraphiti, *and* Juked. *She teaches at the University of Kansas in Lawrence, Kansas, where she lives with her husband and daughter.*

Part Three:
Blurred Lines

*Friendship viewed through a murky lens.
What did we really want to see?*

After Criselda

Kristabelle Munson

My nephew is five years old. He asks, "Are you a boy or a girl?" I smile. "Most people would say I was a boy—if they didn't know me. Your mom says I'm a girl. I mean, I could be both, right?"

I don't want to mislead him. After all, I wear men's clothing and have a crew cut. My answer satisfies him. He goes back to drawing snakes. I cut wrapping paper for a gift for his soon-to-be-born little sister. The only brown-skinned dolls at the toy store were Pocahontas or Jasmine from *Aladdin*. I chose a stuffed panda instead.

If I think about how the world sees me, I hear voices raised in anger and confusion, as if national security is at risk when I use the women's bathroom. This happens more often in the country I was born in. When I visit my cousins, I notice I am the largest person of the female persuasion on the airplane. Most women from my country are petite. The clothing sold in malls never fits me; I shop in the men's section, and my cousins attempt to steer me to the plus-size rack for women. They grin and say, "For you." A shapeless black smock with the label *After Criselda* affixed on the collar is pressed into my hands.

I never knew what to call myself until college. I settled for *butch*. The description seemed to fit. Finding the personal ads in the *Village Voice's* "Women Seeking Women" section gave me hope until I saw the words *no butches* in most of the ads. The days after college were makeshift jobs and looking for air-conditioning.

My heart hurt. If I was in a bar with a jukebox, I spent most of the time selecting sad songs, replaying my last weeks on campus. There was a girl. A dancer. She was my friend first. A straight girl. She was almost mute. She never spoke to anyone else. She told me she needed me for one night. So

I slept with her. For more than one night. There was a problem, of course. She was married to a professor. She wrote letters and ripped them up. I went through her garbage cans and pieced the letters back together with tape. In the letters never meant to be seen I got the proof I wanted. She loved me. She was my friend but she loved me. She put it down in ink. On graph paper.

It ended on graduation day: have a nice life. She turned and walked away. I was used to not hearing her voice because she almost never spoke. But the silence of her body leaving my side? I lost one of my senses. The ability to keep the line between friendship, adoration, love. The graph paper made the ripped-up letters easy to piece together. I looked for the formula of what percentage of bonding, respect, physical desire—what was the alchemy turning friendship to romantic love?

When I left college and moved back to the borough of Queens in New York City, I was lonely. If I went to a bar, it wasn't in search of a date; I was just looking for friends. In the subway, moving through crowds, I smiled at strangers when I wasn't supposed to. I could feel my loneliness grow and thicken. It had its own shadow, its own area code. When I cut my hair to a fuzzy downy baby-chick bristle a homeless man said, "Hey, Buddha, will you bless me?"

I rubbed the top of my head and felt the softness. I gave him a dollar and had enough left over for a bagel. I was beginning to feel invisible in NYC. There seemed to be a pecking order, a hierarchy amongst the masculine gay women. There was a white world and a black world. The white girls went to big dance parties thrown for special occasions. Tickets were twenty-five dollars. There were lounges where the white girls gathered, in restaurants owned by lesbian chefs.

Black lesbians went to Her/She Bar on Friday nights. These parties were thrown by a white promoter but catered to the black and Latino women of New York. Further divisions of class.

Working-class white dykes felt welcome in the East and West Village bars. Black lesbians of every class and social standing were often subjected to the practice of triple carding. Three separate forms of legal identification were demanded from black lesbians for entry to some bars. A driver's license? Okay. Passport and another photo ID? Sorry, you don't have it—can't come in. The Duchess II off Christopher Street, rumored to be Mafia-owned as many of the gay bars were at that time, wanted to change its identity from a black-girls' bar to a white bar. A sudden change in door policy often accompanied management's wish for a different color of clientele.

Meow Mix catered to the riot-grrrl indie-rock queer girls. Henrietta Hudson drew bridge-and-tunnel women looking to hook up before the last train to Long Island. Rubyfruit had oriental rugs and Moroccan lamps for white-lipstick lesbians to cruise beneath.

At a bar on Leroy Street called Crazy Nanny's I met an older girl. She introduced herself as Sean. Faded blue jeans and a crew-neck T-shirt. Pretty but boyish with dirty-blond wavy hair. This was promising. Maybe a new friend. The conversation was easy. Advice for the new kid.

Sean didn't use a glass for her bottle of beer. She could hold up her hand and make the sign for two beers and the bartender didn't ignore her. Outside the bar at two a.m. we shook hands. I started walking toward the East Village and Sean made her move near Allen Street. Her mouth was soft and her tongue met mine. The kissing was the first physical contact I experienced in NYC.

Sean said, "You will do fine." She hailed a cab and got in.

At the end of Houston Street, East River Park skirted the water. There was barely any grass, and unofficial soccer games took up most of the space until the word-of-mouth lesbian touch-football game started up. Let me be clear: it was not touch; this was full-on contact. Games were interrupted by girls being carted off the field with twisted ankles, one broken nose, and one possible concussion. There were femme girls and butch girls. Teams were chosen in the age-old tradition of "I'll take her" and pointing. Some days it was hard to determine if athletic prowess or a good profile led the captains to choose their sides.

Both teams took turns kicking away shards of glass, sweeping up any hypodermic needles. A tall girl named Tara with auburn ringlets and olive skin was a defensive specialist. She had a good vertical leap and impeccable timing. Tara intercepted two passes every Sunday. I was unprepared when she lateraled the ball to me. I didn't drop it, but I was tackled immediately. She was sharp with me. "Hey, Fuzzy, try to run next time. Maybe less doughnuts during the week?" Tara patted her stomach and I ignored her. She was always showing off how many pull-ups she could do on the monkey bars near the field.

After the games we gathered at Tara's apartment on Stanton Street. This was in the days when you needed a Louisville Slugger baseball bat near the front door. Typical conversations with roommates went like this:

"Goin' to the deli for a six-pack."

Roommate: "Hey don't forget the bat!"

Alphabet City on the Lower East Side was still harsh. I didn't notice that my football posse was part of the first wave of gentrification. We didn't own it; we just frequented the bars and the cafés and the new breed of supermarkets.

When Tara first moved into the apartment she only had a radio, so she put on a disco station and the butches and the femmes danced to whatever song came on. I sat in the corner, on the floor, watching. I was the new kid, a few years younger than most of them. When Tara emerged from cleaning up after the Sunday games she was in a tight tank top, tattoos showing, 501 jeans and a thick brown belt. Her olive skin and Persian last name on the doorbell went together. On Father's Day she picked up the telephone and spoke in rapid-fire Farsi to her dad. I don't know what she said.

There were so many dykes on the team, it was always somebody's birthday. One night we went to the Duchess II and our quarterback, AZ, got triple carded. Some of the white girls just wanted to go in, but Tara bitched out the bouncer and started an impromptu protest. When the bouncer relented, Tara said, "Up yours."

That was the night our friendship started. Since I was younger, Tara called me Small Fry even though I was twice as heavy as she was. She lectured me on eating greens, on exercise. I watched Tara lift weights at the Y and run sprints in the park. I made sure to pretend to eat healthy in front of her. Late at night I would think about how hungry I was. How starved I was for everything necessary for a real life.

Tara was a lady-killer. The most gorgeous females were on her arm and in her bed. Tara had theories about how to make girls feel nice and what kind of cologne to wear. She looked like a matinee idol from the fifties. When she was on the prowl, I didn't even qualify as a wingman. I was the water boy. I knew how many ice cubes she liked and to get the hard pack of cigs, not the soft.

The summer passed. A new dance party opened on Friday nights at the space called Mother in the Meatpacking District. In those days meat warehouses lined either side of Fourteenth Street, and men in bloodstained white coats brandished hooks to get the carcasses dressed. At five p.m. the meat packers changed places with the bar backs and the illegal clubs got ready for the night.

An all-night bagel shop fed the ladies of the evening at all hours. The

Old Homestead Steakhouse had a life-size plastic heifer atop the marquee, beaming her munificence to the nightlife denizens looking for underground clubs.

There was a strict queer girls and dykes of any color door policy. Men needed at least two lesbians to vouch for them in order to get in the club. The name of the club had droves of girls at the door. The Clit Club.

At the Sunday touch football game, both teams were looking forward to next Friday at the Clit Club. There were go-go girls, two DJs, strong drinks, a pool table. There was going to be something special this weekend. Something the gay boys had and didn't seem to appreciate.

A real back room.

It was the year every lesbian wanted what the boys had. Complete sexual freedom. They could just walk down the street, flirt, and hook up with a complete stranger. They had carte blanche to get it on with any guy who fancied them. The back room was a place any girl at the Clit Club could visit. If you were in the back room, you meant business.

We talked a lot about it after football. Tara would claim she already was living the gay boy lifestyle 24/7, but all of us knew Tara was partial to one femme girl in particular. They were a serious couple. Lucy had long black hair and always wore miniskirts, even in winter. Okay, she wore tights in winter, but it was still striking to see a looker of a girl in a miniskirt in subzero weather. When Lucy wasn't around, Tara would draw a bubble bath after football and strip off muddy clothes and boxers and get in the tub. It was Lucy's bubble bath stuff, so it smelled pretty girly.

On Friday night I took care with making sure my crew cut was freshly buzzed. I showered and put on sandalwood oil and wondered why, because no one had touched me since Sean's single-serving kiss. But at least I was finding friends. I had that.

The line outside the Clit Club was maddening. It took an hour to get in. The go-go girls were extra mean. They scoffed at dollar bills. They wanted Lincolns or Hamiltons. The faces of new girls at the club, their mouths open and breathing heavy at the pole dancers, pointing at the studs at the pool table. They could learn a thing or two from Tara.

She coolly put a cigarette behind her ear and loped down the basement steps. In the direction of the back room. I followed her because that was what I'd done since I met her. The back room was the old refrigerator room of the building. The door was heavy with a big metal bar for a handle. It was hard to see and smelled musty. My eyes adjusted to the dim red light. I could hear heavy breathing. I couldn't see farther than a foot in front of me.

I leaned against the wall and pressed my palms behind me. Now that I was in the back room, I didn't know what I was supposed to do. Twenty minutes passed. It was time to go.

I'd had the guts to do it. I could say I'd visited the back room if anyone ever asked me.

But before I could move, someone slammed me against the wall. The back of my head was going to have a lump tomorrow. I didn't care.

Tara was on top of me. Kissing me. Hungry for me.

I stayed perfectly still.

Tara used my body for target practice.

Time, that little fucker, he stopped.

And my body ate until it was full.

And the formula I thought about all summer. The graph paper. Friendship plus adoration plus crush plus lust plus disbelief plus the feeling of being alive. I would give anything to feel this. To feel.

Tara never came back to football, and no one questioned me about it because the game broke up shortly afterward. I never saw her again.

I kept the After Criselda shirt in my closet for years until I gave it to a high-end charity thrift shop. I wore it twice. Back in the old country, to make my cousins happy.

Kristabelle Munson's writing has been published in the zine Fat Girl *and in* TAYO Literary Magazine. *Kristabelle is a VONA/Voices fellow and attended the Stonecoast MFA in Creative Writing program. As technical director for the first two years of the Moth, her duties included schlepping heavy lights and microphones to various bars in Alphabet City.*

Le Cahier de Fabienne

Jennifer Lang

After twenty-five years, many of which have been spent at the bottom of a box, the journal has a faint smell of ash. I put it close to my nose and take a deep inhale before opening it.

On the first page, I see her familiar penmanship with its tight slant to the right and start to read in French: *Le cahier de Fabienne pour Jennifer.* Fabienne's notebook to me, a farewell present before I left France.

When I first spotted the two young women walking arm in arm, I knew they were French. It was a game I'd been playing since my junior year of college in Paris, when I learned how to discern Europeans by their clothes, gait, and gestures. Most American women don't walk with their elbows linked or V-neck wool sweaters draped around their necks.

I picked up my pace to close the distance between us and hear them speak just as they stopped to study a Manhattan street map. Without hesitating, I pinched my lips firmly together to sound less American and said, *"Pardonnez moi, puis-je vous aider?"* to see if they wanted help. Taken aback, they giggled. Of the two, the one with the frizzy black hair hesitated, and I could feel her eyeing me. We were somewhere in Greenwich Village, and they were searching for an obscure art gallery.

"Vous êtes d'ici?" The wary one asked if I was from the city. I explained I was a native Californian, in town for a family visit, and currently living in Paris, where the metro, bus, and side streets were more familiar to me than those of New York City. They were wide-eyed, eager to know why I lived in their hometown. Within minutes, we exchanged names and numbers in France so that upon our return we could meet again.

I glide my hand over the soft-covered, smoky black notebook and delight in the feel of its embedded floral pattern; an anonymous poem about hope is engraved in a simple gold twelve-point font. On the sixth and last line, written in English: *I'm sure we should all happy like a queen.* The word *be* is missing and makes me think a French speaker must have accidentally omitted the verb.

Once open, the cream-colored pages strike me as beautiful with their gray lines, bordered frame, and khaki floral backdrop. I turn the page, curious to see what Fabienne wrote, since my memory fails me. In French it reads, "The story starts here," below which is a picture of a hazy gray sky over the Hudson River surrounding the Statue of Liberty and the edge of downtown Manhattan. The photograph was surely taken during her trip—and our chance encounter—in 1987, and the Twin Towers dominate the horizon.

"It continues here," she wrote on the next page, and above it is a photo of a foggy Parisian sky with the Seine River, a Bateau-Mouche under one of the many bridges, and the Eiffel Tower. The word là—"*there*"—stands alone at the top of the following page with a photo of the Seine and the Pont des Arts footbridge and, below it, one of the domes of the Louvre, where Fabienne was studying art. On the next page, she wrote *là* . . . above a photo of an unidentifiable statue in front of an unrecognizable building. Mesmerized, I turn the pages to see and remember—Paris, Fabienne, our friendship—and there's a picture of the Jardin des Tuileries carousel. I cannot recall if any of these places held a certain import for us. All I know is how much I loved that city in its entirety, Fabienne at its center.

As soon as I returned to Paris after my family trip to New York, I called my new French friends. Both twenty, of Moroccan descent, and in college, they each lived with their parents and immediately invited me over for meals. From the outset, Fabienne and I had the stronger bond.

The following Sunday, I rang the bell at her apartment in Versailles, and a heavyset, gray-haired woman with the same frizz atop her head greeted me, opening her arms into a big hug. *"Bonjour! Enchantée, enfin!"* she said as if speaking in exclamations, welcoming me and telling me it was nice to meet me, finally! I instantly saw the mother-daughter resemblance, both dressed in all black with uncontrollable hair, shapeless bodies, round faces, pale skin, and piercing dark eyes. Fanny introduced herself and ushered me in, and I gravitated toward her maternal warmth immediately.

The rest of Fabienne's family stepped forward—Papa, whom I could call by his first name, Moise; and her older brother, Philippe, who was the same age as my brother. The men, in comparison, were more reserved, offering me their cheeks to *faire les bises*.

Since it was too early for dinner, we sat in the living room to talk and sip our *apéritifs*. One after the other, they fired umpteen questions at me. What did my dad do? How old was I when I first started learning French? With my lips puckered and my tongue toward the back of my throat to make my version of a rolled *r*, I answered them all.

That first meal turned into one of many. Single, American and Jewish, I became an honorary family member, commanded to *tu-toi* them, a more familiar way of addressing people in contrast to *vous*. Throughout the next year, I spent almost every Jewish and secular holiday sitting around the table with Fabi and her family: couscous for Friday night Shabbat dinner; *la confiture de coings*, or quince jam, to break the Yom Kippur fast; and non-kosher oysters on New Year's Eve. I was even included in birthday celebrations. Aside from spending long hours at the table, we often watched television or listened to music, sat around drinking mint tea, and just talked.

I continue leafing through the notebook. Unlike me, it hasn't aged in the past twenty-five years. The binding is strong, the pages clean and wrinkle-free, not one crease or show of wear.

After the pictures of Paris, Fabienne wrote, *"This is me since you left,"* next to a postcard of Picasso's *La Femme qui pleure*, a profile of a woman's face, angular with a pointed nose, one eye turned up and a tear falling and another eye on her cheek with two tears. The lips are painted red and streaks of magenta are scribbled on her cheek and down her neck. In true Picasso fashion, she's distorted and disturbing.

I stare at the postcard and recall how broken Fabi was when I moved away. Nearing the end of her degree in art at the École du Louvre, she had no idea if she could find a job in her field or where she would live. Her dream was to settle in Manhattan, where we talked about living together while I went to graduate school and she worked. Since I had at least six months between leaving France and school starting, my plan was to go to Israel, learn Hebrew, and spend time with my brother. Then, we'd agreed, we would meet in New York City.

Fabienne shared everything with me. Not only her family, but also her friends: Val, an Air France flight attendant; Anne-Marie, a designer for Jean-Charles de Castelbajac; and Caroline, from art school. Young Parisian women, they included me in their conversations and extended invitations to parties, dinners out, or art openings. Linking arms as we strolled through the streets of Paris, Fabienne and I became inseparable.

The following pages in the notebook are a mix of Fabienne's philosophical outlook on life and pictures and postcards of Paris and people. One of my most favorites is of the Palais-Royal courtyard, with its modern assortment of black-and-white painted columns of differing heights dotting the open space. I love the juxtaposition of the old and new—there, and at the Pompidou, and the glass pyramids at the Louvre—and she knew it.

Ce dont je rêve . . . , she wrote—"I dream of this"—adjacent to a postcard of a man and a woman in trench coats with briefcases running on a street in Manhattan, circa 1950, with clunky black Buicks and simple skyscrapers in the background.

A postcard of Marc Chagall's Rainbow from 1931, with images of Israel, covers two pages, above which Fabienne wrote, "What we will always share, and what I hope we will find again." I don't understand the reference, since we met in America and shared Paris, not Israel. Maybe she was referring to being Jewish women with connections to the land, or to my imminent departure for Israel.

When I think of my year and a half in Paris, I think of Fabienne. She and I spent so much time together, mostly on foot, roaming our favorite arrondissements. Mine was the 4ème, le Marais and around la Place des Vosges, while hers was the 2ème, all the narrow, winding streets behind the Louvre, a part of the city I had never explored or been interested in prior to knowing her. We spent countless rainy Saturdays sharing sushi and bento boxes at hole-in-the-wall Japanese restaurants, my first foray into East Asian cuisine. Most weekends, we attended museum exhibits or art gallery openings, or simply strolled through outdoor markets, occasionally buying a baguette or a chunk of cheese. Another pastime we shared was the movies—matinees on the weekend and evenings during the week. Together we saw a film about Camille Claudel, an artist who became the mistress of Auguste Rodin, and I indulged her Woody Allen obsession by seeing his movies whenever they were playing.

Page after page I turn, and our closeness comes back to me. So many years later, I know what it means to move and make new friends, to bring someone into your life, fully. Fabienne did it wholeheartedly with me, for me. Her family members along with her three closest girlfriends fill two full pages with photos, a note, their name, and contact information. Even her cat Baba is included.

Before leaving Paris in mid-February of 1989, I invited Fabienne to visit me in Israel a few months later, once I was settled.

After a month at my brother's, I moved in with two friends, an arrangement that suited me well until they had to return to America and I unexpectedly met a Frenchman named Philippe, who lived two hours away in Haifa.

From May until July, we commuted back and forth on weekends. He begged me to live with him, which seemed foolish since I wasn't intending to stay in the country yet irresistible since we wanted to be together every moment possible. Our relationship intensified, leading me to defer my graduate studies in New York, pack up my duffel, and head north.

Fabienne visited me in the midst of my blossoming romance. Since meeting Philippe, I had crammed every thin blue aerogram with sentences starting with "Philippe this" or "Philippe that." By the time I met her at Ben Gurion Airport and we bussed back to our overheated apartment in Haifa, she knew that we each had one older brother who lived in Israel; our parents were the same ages; our favorite color was green; we played tennis, rode bikes and skied; we each spoke several languages and yearned to travel.

If Fabi's eyes glazed over while I confided in her about my boyfriend, I didn't notice. If she was angry or hurt or resentful of his place in my life, I didn't see it. If she felt second or small or sorry she had come to Israel, I didn't realize. All I can recall is that our visit together was intense with deep, philosophical conversations and all-day touring—from the Old City in Jerusalem to the beach in Haifa. At the Jaffa flea market, we bought matching oversized multicolored pants with patterns resembling a Matisse painting. We laughed at our old jokes and talked as if months hadn't passed, confiding our secrets and dreams. And when I bused her back to the airport, we hugged each other hard, unsure of our next visit, where, when, if.

The last few pages in the notebook are filled with artwork and Fabi's feelings, beautiful words that circle around the idea that she will miss me and how special our relationship is. *La tendresse est un art et l'art peut être tendre, comme la, comme nous*—"tenderness is an art and art can be tender, like us."

On the last page, opposite Gustav Klimt's *The Kiss*, in which a dark-haired man embraces a woman, both wrapped in a golden quilt, she wrote something to the effect that as long as our future resembles that of *The Kiss*, *n'est-ce pas?*

Even after all these years, I try to understand the meaning. What was she trying to tell me when she wrote those words, bound them in a book, and handed me before I left Paris? What did I miss then?

About a week after Fabienne returned to Paris, I received a letter. A sealed envelope addressed to me with several pages written in her tightly slanted penmanship and filled with words. Words of contempt. Words that made me cry. That reminded me of being in high school when girls turned on girls. When friendships ended. They were words I read once, maybe twice, possibly again, that I shared with Philippe, until, finally, I threw them away.

Fabienne was finished with me; our friendship of the past almost two years, which now spanned from New York to Israel, mostly anchored in France, was done, as far as she was concerned. I had no more room for her, she claimed; I was too obsessed with my boyfriend, unable to see beyond him. She had decided. I was never asked.

Her words, so hurtful and horrifying, burned me. I hadn't anticipated them and was ill-prepared for them as well as for the sudden loss of her friendship.

At twenty-two, I was uninterested in playing games. I had suffered enough in school, been dumped and turned on, and, in turn, dumped others.

Usually I recognized the gray fluidity in relationships, but for me this was black and white. She was dumping; I was done. I wasn't going to respond to or fight with her or be defensive, neither by phone nor by letter.

I never saw or heard from Fabienne again.

When I flip through the pages of the notebook for the last time, I eye her brother's business card next to his photo. The family's last name, which I had forgotten, jumps out at me.

Without thinking too long or too hard, I open up Facebook and search for her, unsure of her whereabouts. She appears immediately, and I click.

According to her profile, she's been living in Brooklyn, New York, since a few months after she sent me our breakup letter. Save for a few wrinkles and sun spots, she looks the same. Her hair is a mop of black waves that still fly in all directions. She dresses in neutral colors, dangles accessories around her neck, and wears a turquoise stone ring on the fourth finger of her left hand. Relationship status and other details are hidden behind privacy settings. From the handful of pictures that I can see, I don't think she's married. I cannot tell if she's happy and realize I'm not sure she ever was.

I also realize something else that astounds me: I'm not sure if my friendship with Fabienne was based on a sincere and mutual connection as much as it was my deep-seated longing for a French friend, a gateway to that country, its culture and language.

I stare hard at her face and, for the first time, it dawns on me, why she cut me out of her life so drastically all those years ago.

Artsy and eccentric, Fabienne was uncomfortable in her skin, maybe more at ease with women than with men. In all our time together, I had never known her to fantasize about, flirt with, or date anyone.

Perhaps she was in love with me then, I think. When I left Paris and was no longer the center of her world, only to find a man who became the center of mine, she was blinded by jealousy, which turned into rage. She knew she was losing or already had lost me—and there was no chance of getting me back. And while a part of me loved her—as a friend—I might have loved what she represented more.

Which makes me think maybe, like me, Fabienne was also in love with the *idea* of me as her perfect American friend, her gateway to the culture and language of New York—and our relationship skewed on both sides by cultural infatuation.

Toward the end of the notebook, she wrote: "All of my friendship. Ah yes! All of my friendship for you in your dreams and in your heart. Never forget it. Your friend always." In true Fabienne fashion, she spoke around the subject, using a lot of unnecessary words, rather than say things directly.

Sitting nearby in our home office, Philippe turns around to see what I'm doing.

"Do you remember her?" I ask, pointing at Fabienne's picture.

He nods. I show him the black book she made for me and remind him of the letter she sent. He recalls my utter devastation.

"What are you going to do now that you've found her?"

I shrug my shoulders, not knowing. Gently, I glide my right hand over her page and pause on Add Friend. Before I think or realize what is happening, my fingers press.

"What did you do?" Philippe asks. I look at the screen. *Friend Request Sent* flashes before me. I'm stunned, unsure if I acted out of impulse or by accident.

"I don't know. I guess I'll have to wait and see if she's ready to be my friend."

Well, over a month has gone by and I still haven't heard from her.

Jennifer Lang is a freelance writer and memoir-writing teacher who has been published in the Chicken Soup for the Soul *anthologies* Here Comes the Bride *and* The Power of Positive *(2012);* Saying Goodbye: To the People, Places, and Things in Our Lives; *and* South Loop Review, *among others. Her essays have also appeared on* Ducts.org, *the Webzine of Personal Stories, as well as on* Hospital Drive, *the online literary and humanities journal of the University of Virginia School of Medicine. Connect with her at www.opentoisrael.com, her blog about living in a country she never dreamed of calling home.*

A Snowball's Chance

Penny Guisinger

I pointed the tires at the road ahead, though I was crying hard enough that the road wasn't easy to distinguish. The idea of home, if home is the place that cradles our hearts, was also hard to distinguish that day. I was driving toward the house I shared with my husband and our two young children, but felt like I was leaving my heart somewhere else, somewhere behind me. It was in another house, with Kara, the woman I wanted to sleep with.

I wanted her, but I knew that to have her was to risk everything: my house, my family, my reputation. To have her was to start an affair.

Having an affair would not have been a new idea in my marriage. My husband, John, had been having one for months, though I wanted to believe this was different. As I wiped tears out of my eyes so I could see to drive, I told myself that John's behavior with Torey was entirely different from what I wanted to do with Kara.

And it was, really. My husband's behavior with the woman he had started a band with was not, by some definitions, even adulterous. There was no sex or any other physical impropriety. It was purely an emotional infidelity between the two of them, though most women know this can be the worst kind. No, what I wanted with Kara was not that. I wanted her. I wanted her in bed with me. I wanted my mouth on her neck and her hands on my body. I wanted an affair.

Here's the other problem: I can't tell this story in order. When I try to line up the events chronologically, I get turned around in the details and I can't remember what happened first and then next and then last. Did I pass out drunk in Kara's bed after telling her that my marriage was failing before I even went to that bonfire with my kids and couldn't stop calling her from the phone inside that cabin? Or did that come later? Had I spoken of this desire to anyone by the time I let her undo my belt buckle, or did I wait?

When I was five years old, my older brother had a nightmare. Awakened by noises in the house, I got out of bed to find him sitting, hunched over, arms crossed, at the top of our carpeted staircase. Somewhere behind us, our mother was running cold water onto a washcloth. His face was already wet with tears and water—he could not wake up. I sat next to him, and he described the dream he was still having.

"My arms are too long," he said. "They're getting tangled up in everything." In his dream, the only way to control them was to keep them crossed, just as they were still crossed as he told me. He was hunched over, curled into a ball, resting his folded arms on his knees, rocking himself forward and back, crying.

Some stories of love and friendship are like those arms: long and gangly, impossible to control. To unfold a story means to unfold it all the way—to let it get tangled—for each part leads to questions that lead to answers that lead to other parts. My heart, folded up for a long time, got tangled up in Kara's. It would have been easier if I had kept it packed away, like the way my brother kept his arms crossed, protecting his chest, keeping everything where it belonged. Instead, I let it reach out to hers and become entangled. Once that happened, it was impossible to neatly wrap it back up in my chest, in my safe, heterosexual home. Like my brother all those years earlier, I couldn't put a wet washcloth on my face and snap out of it.

Not only was this other woman, Torey, beautiful and skinny and fun; she was also my friend. She had long, thick hair, shampoo-commercial beautiful, and was always laughing and smiling. I outweighed her by at least three pants sizes and was laughing and smiling less and less the longer John and I were married.

"Ted and I are starting a band," she said to me one afternoon when I was at her house with my kids. We had gone over for a playdate, and Torey and I were making lunch. Ted was her equally perfect husband. "We just decided last night. We've always wanted to do it, and so we're just going for it." Her energy, as she said this, was downright bubbly.

In Torey's company, I felt oafish and stumbling, but to my credit I liked her anyway. We shared interests, but not abilities. We both liked to run, but her pace was much faster than mine, her endurance stronger. We liked going to thrift stores, but she always found better things. She was willing to dig deep into the racks, and emerged, every time, with a cute size-two dress or a pair of expensive leather boots marked down to fifty cents. Both our families liked camping and hiking, but she was married to Ted—a registered Maine guide—and their gear was always the right gear, their campsite always more comfortably outfitted. It wasn't that I was trying to compete with her. There was no point in that. Until John fell in love with her. That came later.

"John and I have always talked about starting a band too," I offered, stirring powdered cheese into a pot of hot elbow macaroni. Upstairs, our kids pounded down the hallway, coming downstairs to eat. "We both play guitar and sing." The butter melted and pooled in the macaroni.

She lit up, her already-radiant smile becoming even more radiant. "Ooh, then you should both be in it too!" She pulled a piece of cold cooked chicken from the fridge and picked at it. "That would be so fun." Bubbly.

I watched Torey place that piece of chicken on her plate next to a salad. Just looking at her perfectly portioned balance of carbs and protein made me feel fat. I scooped a spoonful of steaming macaroni and cheese onto my plate, next to my salad, and wondered if I would be skinny and perfect too if I ate meat. Or maybe if I bubbled more. Or had her hair.

I told John about the band idea that night, after our kids were in bed. "It would be you, and me and Ted and Torey and Brian. Maybe the other Brian too." (The Brians were other friends—members of other couples.) We sat in our kitchen, drinking wine, pondering this idea. For years we had talked of learning some songs together, but had never taken the time. Something in our relationship stopped us: some self-consciousness that we couldn't find our way around, some inability to be that vulnerable. This insight comes closer to why we got divorced than any of the plot points in this story. What I know now is that you can't be in love and not be vulnerable. If your heart stays safely curled up in your chest, it will stay safer, but if you can't sing badly in front of your partner, you probably won't be able to ask for his or her support when you lose your job or need help getting home because you drank too much. Without vulnerability, there can be no trust. Without trust, you're never really married.

John was a more experienced musician than I, but I was learning. He had helped me shop for my first good guitar years earlier. We found it hanging on the wall behind the counter at a used instrument shop called Marty's, and I chose it for its Western-inspired design on the pick guard: red flowers and white leaves. "They want to practice on Tuesday nights."

"How would we do that?" John sipped his wine. We had been living in this rural Maine community together for a handful of years. It was the place I grew up. I had family here. Making friends as adults is hard, and I was better at it than he was. I had a growing social circle of other moms. John had not made many friends and was lonely. He asked, "Who would watch the kids?"

He was right—this was a problem. Our daughter, Abby, had just started kindergarten, and had to go to bed at a reasonable time. Rehearsals were to be at Torey and Ted's house, and both of their daughters also went to school in the mornings.

What I said next represents one of the most magnanimous moments of my adulthood, and set in motion the events that would be the death blow to our marriage. I said, "Why don't you start going to rehearsals on Tuesday nights. I'll stay home with the kids." I took a gulp of wine. "You bring home the songs, I'll learn them too, and I'll go to rehearsals when I can." I wanted him to have this, wanted him to make friends.

And that's what we did. Almost. John attended rehearsals with near-religious devotion. And at first I did participate in the way we had designed. I learned a couple of songs and went to a few rehearsals, but most Tuesday nights I stayed home. Over time, I began to look forward to these nights: just me and the kids. We read extra stories or watched a movie together while eating giant bowls of popcorn. Two towns over, I knew that John was having a great time and that my turn would come. This, I thought, was a fine example of my ability to compromise in our marriage. I thought this grand gesture would help us through the wreckage we were becoming. I thought this might be our last chance.

Their first public performance was part of a multiband lineup at a church fund-raiser. It came so soon after John joined the band that they played without me. I hadn't had time to learn the songs. Because the church was just a couple of miles from our house, I offered to host a party for us all afterward.

The church fund-raiser was what anyone would expect a church fund-raiser to be like. The seats were uncomfortable pews, the sound in the high-ceilinged room was awful, and the audience was composed of overdressed people with gray hair. The band, now named Snowball's Chance in Heck, delivered their three-song set in between the local Celtic group and a subset of the church choir. I sat with the wife of one of the Brians. All our kids were there. I have a photograph of my plump, bald infant son in his little seat in the aisle with Torey's youngest daughter. They are both grinning. There were no surprises. No mistakes.

Back at our house, John and I shoved bottles of beer into an icy cooler. "I thought you all sounded great," I offered.

He grinned. He agreed, seeming so happy to have had this chance.

Arriving a bit later, Torey dramatically plopped herself into an over-stuffed chair and, with an eye-rolling glance at her band, said airily, "I'm so sorry guys. Remind me never to book another *church gig* again."

John, Ted, and both Brians, with bottles of beer in their hands, all nodded in assent. Nobody smiled at her obvious overstatement. "Oh, yeah," said one of the Brians. "That was brutal."

Deep in my brain, an alarm bell went off. Her language had shifted over the past weeks. They hadn't committed to play some songs at the fund-raiser. Instead, they had *booked* a *gig*, where they would play some *tunes*. (Torey went on, in later years, to introduce every song onstage as a tune. As in "We're going to do a little Steve Earle tune for you now." The word still sets my nerves on edge.) I tried to ignore the blaring alarms.

I performed with them at their first "big gig"—at a restaurant and bar in a neighboring town. I chose a couple of songs, and managed to make time to practice with the full group a couple of times. These practices felt awkward. When I stepped behind the microphone in Ted and Torey's cav-ernous living room, I had the sense that I was walking in on a party I wasn't invited to. I persisted, not knowing that my career as a member of Snowball's Chance would be limited to this one night.

I took the stage that night, shaking. The band had been playing for maybe an hour by then in an area of floor that was used for performing. The windows behind us were draped in white dangling lights, and the eclectic, yard-sale-style decor of the bar surrounded us. We knew almost everybody in the place. I closed my eyes, tried to stop the trembling, tried to keep it out of my voice. Gripping the microphone like a drowning person holds on to a life raft, I let my nervousness out in the form of a stupid, too-large grin. I let go of the microphone for a moment, shook my hands and arms quickly, let the excess energy out through my fingers, and sang my two songs while the band played loosely behind me. In later years, I would learn the difference between performing on a stage where you're welcome and one where you're not. It turns out that nobody should sing with a backup band that doesn't have their back.

Nobody heard me. Our friends and my family were in the audience. The place was packed. But the sound system went down for the seven minutes it took to sing my two songs. I knew it was happening, as it was happening, but it seemed that nobody else in the band noticed. The "sound guy" (one of the Brians) was also the mandolin player, and had left the board to play his instrument. That sensation of singing into a dead microphone became the theme of what was left of my marriage.

Later, at the post-gig party, I overdramatically said to Torey, "That was such a *nightmare*." We were in a motel room, and I was in a vinyl-covered chair by the generic circle of table. Torey sat on the edge of one of the beds, facing me. We both clutched beer bottles.

She patted my arm. "I'm sorry it was such a nightmare for you." She emphasized that word—*nightmare*—with full awareness of my ridiculousness.

It wasn't the performance I was talking about, but I didn't know that yet. Something about this, all of this, felt wrong. I didn't stay long at the party. I want to say that John and I left together, that he put his arm around me as we walked to the car, but the truth is that I don't remember.

There was a night, sometime in the middle of all this, when John and I went to the movies. We parked the car and walked toward the doors of the theater, and his hands were in his pockets. He cocked his elbow toward me, jauntily inviting me to slip my arm through his. I did it—let our arms entwine—though by that time I was in love with Kara.

I want to say that he did something like that as we were leaving the party, that somehow he knew that my heart was retreating, fast and intractable, behind my rib cage. I want to think that he wanted to do something about it, to change the history that was happening right in front of us. But I believe I drove home alone.

After a short time—just a matter of weeks—John stopped bringing home songs. I stopped feeling comfortable at occasional rehearsals. Sometime later, in the middle of an argument, I asked him outright if I was welcome in the band.

His reply was, "Ted says you don't add anything."

I did not go to another rehearsal.

I have carried my friendships with women across decades of highway, protecting and nurturing these fragile-but-essential entanglements, wielding them like both shields and weaponry against life's onslaughts. I have referred to my closest friends as my "committee"—the people I gather close for decision making, celebration, or grieving. "Friendship marks a life even more deeply than love," wrote Elie Wiesel, and he was right, but he did not stop there. He added, "Love risks degenerating into obsession; friendship is never anything but sharing." I was thrilled to call Torey my friend—thrilled in that she's-amazing-and-I-love-that-she-even-talks-to-me way—but I was less thrilled when the things we began to share grew to include my husband.

Torey and I performed together at an event called Chicks with Picks. Held in a student lounge at the state university in Machias, Maine, the event was a fund-raiser for the domestic-violence organization where I worked as assistant director. It was an open mic, exclusively for women. I can't tell you, all these years later, the name of the song we did, only that it was about women and athletes, Diana Nyad, and being strong. We practiced it in my living room with an improvised sound system involving a microphone and a guitar amp. We took the stage that night, in front of all the college girls in their sweatshirts and jeans, and Torey sang while I accompanied her on guitar. They loved us. I loved her. She loved the attention.

Our friendship somehow limped through the indignities of all that was going on, though I was holding on tighter than I should have.

There were other performances. Snowball's Chance played at a fund-raiser for the county Democrats. I played too—alone. They played at an event for the community learning center—on the sun-drenched deck overlooking the bay—and John and I practiced a song to do together with the band. Characteristically, they finished their set and left the stage after forgetting to invite me up. Torey apologized as we sat facing each other, drinking giant frosty beers in the sun. I dashed two shakes of salt into my drink, and watched the crystals dissolve as they sank into the amber. I forgave her. Again. And then again.

How could I not forgive my gorgeous, laughing friend? Torey was the girl I had wanted to have as my friend since high school. She was the popular girl, not the girl I was. She was not the girl who shot pictures of basketball games for the school paper or who sat up late at night writing reams of terrible fiction. That's the girl I was. She was also not the prom queen, because who wants to be that? She was the girl who got her license first, and who drove around with a few chosen girls in the backseat, and they all smoked cigarettes but still got straight As. I had always wanted this girl as my friend, had always wanted that particular light to shine on me, and now that it was, I didn't want to share it. At least not with my husband, though I understand that he had always wanted a girl like that too.

There were warnings that I could have chosen to pay more attention to. The wife of one of the Brians (the Brian who ran 10Ks) tried to tell me, almost in code, one night in my own kitchen, while the others were in the living room, that Torey was well aware of her powers. She tried to tell me, without telling me, to watch out.

"Marriage is really hard" is almost what she said. "It's great when they have friends, but you might want to pay attention." Her Brian had become Torey's running partner for a time, and had become strangely dedicated to his sport.

I was making something, pouring drinks or popping popcorn, and I thought, *That's you. It won't happen to me.*

I wonder, still, what it must be like to have that sort of pull on people. What a powerful animal attractiveness is. To those who have it, it must feel like a drug. If I had it, I would want to exercise it, let it run itself out at the end of a lead, galloping around and around the paddock. Or I would want to use it, to inject it into my veins, let it take me into my head and away from all this. I wonder what "all this" Torey was trying to escape as she let us revolve around her like moons. She knew she had gravity.

It was in that context that I started playing music with my new friend Kara. We met at a potluck, shared an Indigo Girls song (because some stereotypes are just true), and started practicing at her house, sometimes late at night, with lots of wine. She was five times the musician John or Torey would ever be, and it pleased me that they knew it too.

On the day of the drive home, the one with the crying, Kara and I had been practicing. We had a gig coming up, and had spent that afternoon with guitars strapped on, running through our songs. We stood in the warm sun in her dining room, all polished oak and golden-colored fabrics and candles and stones. The sun poured in, molten, through the giant windows that overlooked the deck that overlooked the field and forest that was the yard. Its rays ignited the room. Our voices pushed into each other's, in harmony. Kara was classically trained. Harmony lines came easily to her, but they were hard work for me. To teach me a harmony line, Kara would record herself singing it so I could practice it alone in the car on the drive back to my house. I spent many miles, during this time of our relationship, singing the same chorus over and over again, trying to learn the counterintuitive rises and falls of the harmony line. Melody is seductive in its familiarity, and part of learning harmony is forgetting melody. Our relationship took on that characteristic of forgetting and relearning, letting go and reclaiming.

When we finished practicing that afternoon, I packed up my guitar and my three-ring binder full of songs, and drove home. At this point, Kara and I had been playing music long enough to have a repertoire. Our first "big gig" had been in that same restaurant and bar where my nightmare performance had taken place, and we were invited to open for Snowball's Chance. The invitation was made, and accepted, in the spirit of reconciliation. John was relieved that I had this new musical relationship in my life, and I was relieved to have something to distract me from how shitty our marriage had become. John's obsession with Torey was not abating, and I lived with that constant humiliation and a growing realization that I might just spend the rest of my adult life alone, but still in this marriage. He was spending his hours working out chord progressions to accompany Torey's lyrics while I was at work, earning a living. Plot point: I had ambitions in life. I had a master's degree and a job. I didn't know exactly where we were going, but I was committed to making sure we went somewhere. John's temperament was an artistic one, tempered by depression, and he worked part-time for our entire marriage. His own ambitions to become an artist, to get his paintings off the easel and out of the studio and into some galleries somewhere, never seemed to get his attention. He was too busy. He was in a band, and there was Torey to attend to.

Sometimes, it's more complicated than greener-looking grass on the other side of a fence. Sometimes, that other grass over there makes you realize that the grass under your feet has been brown for years and that it's not coming back.

Kara's grass was definitely green. She had a master's degree and a full-time job. She was regularly making me dinner before we practiced. As my feelings for her developed—my attraction, those flashes of desire, the need to be in her company more and more often––the other part of my brain, the logical part, started stacking these qualities she had up against those that John lacked. I was attracted to her long hair and soft shoulders, but also to her competence, her steadfastness.

"Kara, I'm curious," I said to her late one night. "Are you a lesbian?" We sat, guitars across our laps, and if I had known how to pray I would have been beseeching the heavens for a no. If she was straight, like I was supposed to be, the possibility of there ever being an "us" would go away.

But her answer was, "Yes. I'm gay." She looked me in the eyes as she answered. I don't know if she knew why I needed to know when I did.

John was spending a lot of time on the phone with Torey. I was working full-time, and he wasn't, so I couldn't be entirely sure how often they spoke, but I would call home, midday, to find the phone busy—for hours. I knew exactly who he was talking to. It's one of the great unstudied mysteries how wives know this stuff, but we do. Even when I was home she would call, and he would take the cordless phone upstairs to talk. There was a lot of quiet chuckling on his end of the phone.

I tried to be stoic about this. I tried to be cool and understanding about his close friendship with this gorgeous, fun, laughing woman, because she was also my friend and I trusted her. Even when I was in the throes of feeling miserable about our largely sexless marriage, I tried to be the kind of person self-assured enough not to feel threatened. John and Torey had found a musical kinship. That was all. They were writing songs together.

"She's an amazing writer," he said to me over dinner. "Just amazing."

Snowball's Chance was getting gigs. They played that same restaurant multiple times and scored other venues as well. They developed a small following with Torey at the microphone and my husband on lead guitar.

"It's so obvious you have a thing for her," I hurled at him during an argument. Snipped conversations were turning, more and more frequently, into full-on fights. They never ended with any resolution, instead crashing to a halt when I stormed out of the room.

I consoled myself with glasses of wine—way too many—over those many months. In fact, Tuesday nights became the nights when I made regular stops at the store for a bottle of Pinot Grigio on the way home from work. I always left it in the car, hiding it, until he drove away. I spent those evenings with my kids, just as before, but there was always a glass in my hand as I read them stories or made the popcorn. By the time John came back, later and later at night, then earlier and earlier into the hours of the next morning, the bottle was with the other empties in the basement, and I was lost to a drunk sleep.

He denied his "thing" for Torey, told me I was being ridiculous. "This is about you and your insecurities," he said, barely looking up from his guitar. "This is not about me."

One night, when John was working late, I sat alone in the kitchen, drinking. I called Torey, just to chat, just to take a barometer reading, just to test her membership in my committee. The conversation lacked sparkle. I am sure now, looking back, that my voice was monotone at best, colored with suspicion at worst, and that she was in a hurry to get back to her perfect evening. And I thought of Kara. Not just of her bare shoulder peeking out from beneath the strap of her tank top, and not just of her competent, feminine fingers on the strings of her guitar, but of how she looked at me with interest when I talked about literature and politics, when we lifted and set down full then empty wineglasses; how we laughed; how the conversation sparkled.

I made a decision. I was done being married to John.

Kara was out of town when I told him the news. She was traveling with her best friend on a long-planned, two-week trip to the Grand Canyon. We had said good-byes and made uncertain plans to talk or e-mail whenever she found cell signal or Internet access, knowing it might not happen much, if at all. And we made a plan for me to tell my husband that I was in love with someone else. That I was now regularly taking my clothes off with and for someone else. That I had allowed a friendship to degenerate into obsession. That I was now the one having an affair.

I did not equate this with John's "thing" for Torey. In my mind, he fell in love with someone else while we were still together. By the time I fell in love with Kara, he and I had been over for a long time. In his mind, perhaps we were over long before any of it. Maybe, to him, we had never really begun.

I don't believe that he and Torey ever slept together. She was too in love with Ted to jeopardize it all for an afternoon delight with my husband.

Extramarital sex was all my department, in the end, but somehow I convinced myself that his emotional infidelity was worse because it came first.

John and I sat in the kitchen, and the kids were in bed. At least, I was sitting. He may have been leaning his back against the counter or the sink. I was sitting on a bar stool at the narrow, small table that served as an island in the expanse of our kitchen floor. We both held mugs of hot tea.

We were not arguing, but had fought so many times before this moment. We had hurled words, rattled them against each other like sabers, stalked away from arguments, and then come back together, resolving to do better. We had taken these fights to the brink of decision, time and time again, but slunk away when we stared into the gaping chasm of what a separation meant for our kids. Holidays apart, summer vacations split in two, someone always missing out on something, dividing up the Legos, the animals, and Candy Land.

I said, "We need to do something about us." I was ready. I had a solution. He did not ask what I meant. This topic was always in the room. "I know."

"I think we can split up, but do it differently than most people." I was calm. Practical. Like I was discussing a strategy for car shopping or repairing the furnace. I had thought about this. "We can put the kids first and create something that works for them." I went on to describe some utopian scenario in which we built an addition onto our house—an apartment for one of us to live in. I fed these fantasies, in myself, for a couple of years after the split, still believing that we could do this better than most people. In the end, we really didn't. We were revealed as being entirely average in our divorce.

He agreed. "I think we need to do that. All of it. We can't do this anymore."

A marriage that took years to build saw its finality in the time it took to drink one cup of tea.

I let myself into John's computer. It was really our mutual computer, but because I had a laptop from work that I used for everything, the clunkier desktop had become mostly his. I did it one of those nights when he was at practice, and I was drunk on white wine. The kids were asleep, and I was as alone as I had ever been. The bottle had been empty for hours, already rinsed and hidden in the basement, my glass stuck upside down on the top rack of the dishwasher. I didn't know what I was looking for, only that I would know it if I saw it. And I saw it.

John had paid to have an astrologer somewhere conduct a comparison of his natal chart and Torey's. When most people refer to their astrological sign, they're talking only about their sun sign. A full chart is a snapshot of where every planet in the solar system was at the moment of a person's birth: every planet is in one of the signs. John's interest in these matters ran deep. He often tried to explain my own sometimes confounding behaviors by reminding me that my sun and moon signs (Libra and Aries, respectively) were oppositional to each other, creating psychic tension in my brain and heart, making it hard for me to think. I sometimes found him perusing his own chart, looking for clues to his future, to his own head. The comparison of charts he purchased, a practice known as synastry, overlays one person's chart with another's as a way of assessing all the potentialities of their relationship. New lovers should, perhaps, do this as a way of opening a conversation. Long-time couples could do this also, to explore some of their ruts, their existent dynamics. And it seemed that songwriting partners could do it, perhaps, to cross further into the land of inappropriateness.

In his e-mail, I found the report from the astrologer. In the sent folder, I found that he had forwarded the report to Torey. There was no reply from her, but this was in keeping with the complete lack of any record of correspondence between them. He had deleted it all but this one thing, this one telling thing. I turned off the computer, staggered to bed, and fell into my traditional Tuesday night stupor.

It wasn't long after that that Torey pulled the plug. The synastry had been too much for her, it seemed, and she told him over the phone that it all needed to stop. He told me this one evening in the kitchen. "Torey kind of called me out on the whole crush thing" was as close as he came to ownership of what had gone on.

A couple of weeks after that (or perhaps it was months or a year), I went to Torey's house alone, determined to save the friendship. She and I sat outside in the cool New England autumn weather and drank red wine from coffee cups. She told me how uncomfortable the astrology thing had made her, and I worked with her that night to make the whole thing his fault.

"I can't believe it," she said to me when we were nearing the bottom of the big bottle. "I can't believe you even want to talk to me."

We were sitting under blankets on her front porch, facing the dark yard.

Beyond that, the woods loomed skyward toward stars we weren't looking at. "I don't think it was your fault," I assured her. "I think it was all him." The folly of this is only clear now, all these years later, with the ink on our divorce agreement long dry and both of us now living with other partners.

"Do you love him?" she asked.

I took a long drink from the cold rim of my mug, letting the wine wash the truth back down my throat. What I said was, "It's freezing out here. Should we go in?"

There was, of course, leftover business from the conversation in the kitchen. I had left out some details. I had left out the part where I had unfolded the futon in our sun room and let Kara remove my clothes while John and the kids were asleep upstairs. I had left out all the parts where I had called home, claiming to be too tipsy to drive home after practice, and so I was sleeping over at Kara's. I was crawling into her bed and spending those nights learning all the contours of her body.

Three days after the first final conversation, I initiated another one. In my memory, we are in the same positions: me at the table with my feet resting on the low rung of the bar stool, and John leaning against the sink.

I said, "There's one more thing."

He waited.

I said, "When Kara gets back, we're going to . . . ," and here my memory falters. What verb did I use to describe what Kara and I were going to do when she got back? Become openly involved? Start dating? Admit to ourselves and you and everyone else that we're already walking into walls with this love we're in? Whatever I said, he understood.

In fact, what he said was, "I know."

And of course he knew. Husbands, it turns out, have that same gut instinct about their wives.

He added, "I think Kara's great. And I think you deserve it." He wished me the best. This conversation took even less time than the first one.

It's amazing to me now how easily we let it all go, how easily we slid into this life apart, a life in which our kids have to do all the traveling between our homes. Like the way it's easy to slip your arm out of your husband's when you reach the ticket counter and it's time to dig money out of your purse. You just let go.

Now the arms are unfolded – allowed to tangle around each other. I wish I could use them to keep me warm, to make me feel held, rather than just feeling like my chest is exposed, my heart vulnerable. Here, with both arms opened, it makes sense why I cried all the way across that twenty-mile drive home from Kara's house on that Sunday. I was practicing out loud the words I knew I had to say to her. "I swear to you that if I could put this conversation off for even five more minutes, I would." But I knew, that day and it turned out to be true, that to speak those words out loud, to her or anyone else, meant that nothing would ever be the same again. The risk had texture – it was something sharp and hard like a blade. To say to her, "I can't stop thinking about you. I think I might want you," would be to plunge that blade into the rest of my life and rend it apart. And I knew it, and that knowledge is what had made me cry those twenty or so miles past the tidal flat and the trail heads and the post office and the gas station.

I did not know it that day, or for at least a year, that Torey and I would no longer be friends. In the weeks that followed my break-up with John, and in the months that followed those weeks, Torey revealed herself to be one of the friends who chose sides. It took time for me to notice that John was at Torey and Ted's house for dinner regularly, and I was not. There were no calls placed from her house to mine, and after a short time calls in the other direction stopped too. It took years for me to feel anything other than even more oafish and stumbling in her presence, and when it happened it had nothing to do with weight or competence or who was in a band with whom: it was about being happy. When I eventually went on to settle into a life and a love that delivered this simple ingredient, and I encountered her at an event or a party, she didn't seem quite as perfect, quite as untouched. There was no hole for her to fill anymore.

I eased the car through the gentle right turn onto the road that led to my house and pulled myself together. I wiped any remaining tears off with the back of my hand and the sleeve of my jacket. As I made the sharp turn into my driveway, my house came into view. It sat up on a hill and the approach always made it look taller than it was. It stood tall over the car as I climbed the driveway. Some local people were known to call my house "Shingle Mountain," as it was wrapped completely in cedar shingles, even the roof. To me, this ragged wooden skin gave the house a groundedness: like a very old tree. The house felt rooted to the place where it sat. I parked the car by the ell, where the kitchen was located behind rough cedar shakes, turned off the engine and wished that my heart would grow arms – arms that could wrap themselves around this place where I believed I belonged, but where I could not stay.

Penny Guisinger lives and writes on the easternmost tip of the United States. Her work has appeared in Fourth Genre, River Teeth, Solstice Literary Magazine, Under the Gum Tree, Exit 7, *and* About Place Journal. *Her essay "Coming Out" was a finalist in the 2013 Fourth Genre Steinberg Essay Contest, and another essay called "Provincetown" was named an Editors' Pick by* Solstice. *Her work will appear in a second anthology this year. She is the founding organizer of Iota: The Conference of Short Prose. Penny is a graduate of the Stonecoast MFA program at the University of Southern Maine.*

Just Say No

Melody Breyer-Grell

"I have to tell you something and you are not allowed to tell a soul."

I was intrigued and wary as the same time. When Helen made a proclamation like that it could mean someone's head was on the chopping block. We were the bullies of the dog park. Two middle-aged women, sitting around as if bonded by blood, whispering and judging all, often cackling and rolling our eyes as the others wondered what we were cooking up. Who do we have to hate now?

"I am in love with Marcus."

"Marcus, wow, that is nice; he is very cute and funny; you have good taste," I said with completely false sincerity.

"So really, you approve? Think I have a chance?"

What was I to say? This woman had been my best friend for the better part of five years and I had a lot of emotion and time invested in her. And now she was asking me to do the near impossible. She was asking me to lie. I am a terrible liar, not for moral reasons, but because I have a complete lack of discipline and composure when it comes to such things.

This confession of Helen's, her sudden love for Marcus, of all people, really put me on the spot. They were about as compatible as a walrus and butterfly, him being the butterfly. She was a loud, brassy bleached blonde, round and raucous, a bag lady type with six cats and an apartment that was one animal short of a *Hoarders* episode. He was a slim Yogi type, surrounded by pictures of birds and industrial art, a man who was still friends with his ex-girlfriends, the most recent one being a French ballet dancer. Really. I was in deep shit trying to dodge this bullet. I needed a Valium. Or better yet, a joint.

"Of course, I don't see why you wouldn't have a chance, do you?"

"Good, I am glad. I didn't know how you would feel."

What I was feeling was scared. I had imagined that Helen was "retired" and no longer looked at herself as a sexual being. My husband, Allan, my unreasonably tolerant partner of twenty-five years, always wiser about these matters, occasionally asked me if Helen had taken herself "off the shelf." To which I would reply: "Look, she does not even comb her hair, not that I do, but I do have a husband who would have to give me half of what he owns to get rid of me."

"Take it all; I just want my bike," he would counter.

Helen was his fault. Some years ago, Allan had announced delivery of Helen into our world, via a cell phone call while he was outside cycling.

"There is a woman coming over, she said she just got her dog Coco because of our dog Dora and she knows you, so I told her to come over and show you the puppy."

"Someone is coming over here? Now? Who? I am not dressed. What the fuck is wrong with you?"

"She should be over within an hour."

"Thanks a lot, a-hole."

"Kissie."

"Kissie."

My life at that time was very small. I had lost my desire to pursue professional jazz singing, a career even the Man of La Mancha would have considered foolhardy. Any other man might have divorced me for my foibles, but as a man of science, Allan figured he could solve all the world's problems, even mine. I was barely in touch with my former colleagues. Unconnected, I filled too much empty space with pills, pot, and Dora. I tried to keep busy training her, being a supermom to her rather than feeling my loneliness.

That afternoon I met Helen and her dog, Coco, and before I knew it she, Allan, and I were a platonic threesome. She would come over several times a week, like in a sitcom, just ringing the bell and bursting in without calling ahead. Many evenings were lost to junk food and crap-talking. We lazily frittered our evenings away, mostly making fun of our dogs. Dora was strikingly symmetrical, with a polished steel color and tan tuxedo, resembling a small forest animal, ears pointed and nose quivering at stimuli.

Coco was like the homely friend. Her head was too small for her rather thick body and she had a bit of a desperate air around her, often nudging folks with her wet nose. I grew to love the clown. She was funny and goofy with oversized paws and a huge tail. Dora used to sexually abuse her until Coco got bigger. She forever would be able to control the now-pouting Dora. It was a lot of fun.

I became seriously addicted to Helen and pretty much allowed her organize our social life. She was funny and quick, always having a topical comeback for any subject one might put out there. She ruled the dog park, and if you made an enemy of her, you had one for life. Whenever she had a negative proclamation she would light up a cigarette, put her left hand on her generous hip, and screw up her face in a most unbecoming way.

"There she comes, that fucking giant Hutch," regarding a rather tall, large-boned woman for whom Helen had an unreasonable and violent hatred. I was angry at the Hutch too, due to an ill-advised vacation we had embarked upon once. She had been driving and wouldn't stop for me to get something to eat as my blood sugar was plummeting. We had locked horns, but I was ready to end the hostilities and go benign on the subject.

Not Helen, who was just starting. The tall women's "crimes" usually had to do with a tactless but meaningless criticism of Helen's treatment of Coco, including "Hey, Helen, why don't you show Coco more affection?" Or "Did you give her candy again? It's so bad for them. It makes me want to cry."

Well, the Hutch was about to cry too, but not about Coco's diet. Helen would try to dissuade anyone from befriending her and also attempted to get her banned from our get-togethers.

That poor Hutch would wander around asking people, "Why does Helen hate me?" Even when she apologized for her alleged insults, she was never able to win back Helen's goodwill.

I have never been particularly successful in any group of people, possibly due to my intensity, boundary-breaking probes, low tolerance for small talk, or, as some might call it, my bipolar flair. This was the first time I was enjoying a group of people, because with Helen as alpha, and the help of some grass, alcohol, and painkillers, I was now looking forward to people's dull conversations and the social rituals of the day. "Come on, foodies, talk about your recipes, yes, that is a lovely pair of earrings you have on, where did you get them, yes, I love Trader Joe's, their frozen brown rice bowl is the best!" And so on. With Helen's protection, and my stash, I was able to avoid actually doing anything productive and began to fancy myself a "party girl."

A short time after I befriended Helen, I met Rick at one of the bars we frequented for our dog-park get-togethers. I had a drink, smoked some grass, and felt very adorable. He was sitting with his friend Marcus (Helen's future fixation, whom I had not yet met), and I plopped down next to them, attracted to the avuncular vibe that Rick sent out. Blondish and mild, he had a good sense of humor and knew how to make a girl feel comfortable. I was almost hoping he would come on to me, but he was uninterested in any of that. Fully safe in my marriage vows, we became friends, and I liked to walk around the park with him, getting high and spouting off my stories.

No topic was off our list. Especially if it had to do with sex.

"So who do you think is doing who in the park?" he wondered.

"Well, I just found out that Harry is seeing Mary."

"Really? Which one is she?"

"You know, the skinny blonde with the two poodles."

"Are you sure they have done it?"

"Yes, you want pictures?" I laughed.

"How about Helen, is she doing anyone?"

"Nope," I sighed, careful not to mention her obsessive crush on Marcus.

Later, at home, the phone rang. Helen's check-ins about Marcus had become a regular and less than comfortable part of my daily life.

"What do you think he is doing today? Do you think he is seeing anyone?" she interrogated me.

"Absolutely not, no way . . ."

"You sure? How do you know?" Helen demanded.

"Well, I haven't see him with anyone, except his ex, and you told me she has a new boyfriend."

"She does, and he is twelve years younger than her."

"Well, she certainly does not need Marcus anymore. You know I think he is gay altogether," I concluded.

"Ha, well, I will see you tonight."

Allan and I waited for her but she did not show up. The next night, unannounced, she did, totally unbalancing our weekend. Why did I allow this? I thought I was being "mature" by putting up with Helen's peccadilloes. I had spent much of my life discarding friends, not able to tolerate anything but perfect adherence to my desires, and I was going to make this relationship stick.

She was not to be argued with, anyway. I was powerless in her hands. And I needed her.

The winter holiday parties were imminent, and Helen was getting ready to make her move.

"I am gonna put him under some mistletoe and take his little body and shove it against the wall, take some brownies, and—"

"I get the picture," I placated her, actually trying not to picture it at all.

The night of the Christmas party I was stoked. The whole gang would assemble at Harry's apartment and there would be a special gin and cucumber drink called Pimm's Cup. The weed would be plentiful. Helen arrived, transformed. She had blown out her hair, put on contacts and a full face of makeup. She bustled around the kitchen, directing Marcus at the bar.

I was gently baked, and my Pimm's Cup hath runneth over.

"Come here, Helen, I love you," I slurred, attempting to hug her—experiencing a rare flash of loving warmth.

"Yeah," she said distractedly, "let's go out and have a cig."

We lit up a couple of Marlboro Lights (I had dangerously resumed smoking again, despite all the reasons not to), and Helen started to review all the theoretical considerations regarding her attainment of Marcus's affection. As I was shivering and smoking, I tried to back my claims as to why he should like her, but like a torture victim being waterboarded, I made some disclaimers as well. Maybe it would *not* all work out, but that was just because of bad timing and whatnot. As my discomfort grew, I returned to the party.

In an attempt to regain my party mood, I engaged Marcus in a risqué musical discussion, intentionally flirtatious as I laughed, "I only get turned on if there is a Wagnerian prelude playing. Am I a self-hating Jewess?" I just wanted my buzz back. Instead Marcus became serious.

"Well, the girl I have been seeing does not like music and I just don't get it," Marcus said, puzzled.

Girlfriend? How did we miss that? I mulled over how I was going to inform Helen of this development. I knew I was damned if I did and screwed if I didn't, especially if she inevitably learned it from another source.

We dog-park people, we knew how to party, and I had a great time even though I was less than happy to learn Marcus's status. Maybe he meant a former girlfriend, I rationalized. He said it so fast; maybe I got the whole thing out of context. Not likely.

I called Helen the night after the party and I felt something was off right away—she was very cold as I avoided the most salient topic and instead recited my Hurricane Sandy woes, namely having to board my father while his Long Island residence was being overhauled.

"Well, take care of your father. I think we need a break from each other for a while, anyway."

"Why?" I panicked.

"You have been saying some nasty stuff about me and I really cannot deal with that right now."

"What did I say?" I pleaded, mentally going over a list of my recent commentary, not being able to come up with a single friendship-busting statement.

"Well, if you don't know that makes it even worse. People agree with me."

What people? I thought, as I honestly did not recall anything offensive. I was losing control of the situation, one that was apparently of my own making, but one I was clueless over.

"Helen, please, I don't know what you are talking about."

"It won't be forever; just give me time."

"Helen!" The phone went dead.

I was so hurt and furious by Helen's expulsion that I manically called Rick the next day and suggested we take a therapeutic walk, circling the park, hiding a joint.

"So Helen said she is not speaking to you."

"Oh yeah, well, I got some news for you, she is in love with Marcus, and I don't know if I was giving her the encouragement she wanted, or something, but she cut me off for no reason."

"I am going to take that information, put it in a little box with a key, and try to forget about it," he said, apparently disturbed by the images of my now former friend's desired coupling with his bud.

But curiosity got the best of him as I dished out the whole story, including that Marcus might be seeing someone new.

"In two weeks you will be laughing about all this," he concluded.

"Nope, I am finished with her, fuck her, I don't need to be terrorized."

I stumbled home, once again high, feeling guilty about everything, having trouble breathing and wondering what I was going to cook for dinner.

As all had predicted, Helen eventually called me, finally wanted to clear the air.

"So what did I say? I still don't know."

"That remark about if we"—she and Marcus—"met each other thirty years ago maybe I would have a chance."

I did not fully remember saying that, but I explained that if I did, I was not talking about her aging or her looks—just that it might have been simpler back then, before everyone had their difficult life experiences. I had probably just gone on about all that because I had run out of things to say. I might have just been high, no filter, no recall.

Either way, I could not win with this woman, and somewhere, not so deep down, I'd always known our relationship would sour, and it would be ugly. The woman was a borderline personality who could not admit her limitations and I was a bipolar substance abuser who wallowed in mine. The mix was ultimately combustible.

We agreed to resume our relationship, but I was now always on guard and very careful during our phone sessions.

I did start to relax a bit, and then I got *the* call.

"By the way," Helen cooed with feigned indifference, "did you ever tell Rick about my feelings for Marcus?"

"No, of course not," I lied shakily.

"You're sure of that?"

"Yes, sure, I did not tell him. He is not interested in gossip—he is a man."

"Do you swear?"

"No, I don't swear. I did tell him!" I felt I was leaving my body as I spoke. "I thought you dumped me and I was in despair," I exaggerated. "Look, no matter what I say now, you are not going to accept it, and this conversation will end badly, right?"

"Why do you have such a big mouth, going around blabbing my business? I never talk about you. I like to keep my business to myself."

Finally, definitively, she made her ultimate proclamation: "If I see you on the street I will give you a polite hello, but we are done."

My big mouth? Sure, but *hers* was legendary, a thought I had to lessen the sting of my own responsibility in this. I was not going to call her on it. I let her hang up the phone and then experienced a rush of euphoria, realizing that I was as rid of her as she was of me. I came to believe that she was just bored with me and ready to move on. Now she had a reason.

I found myself uninvited to parties that I would have normally gone to, my euphoria evaporating as I sunk into a deep depression, as it was clear I was erased from her consciousness—basically left to find a new identity. Some old friends and family came clean, stating that they had been waiting for the day I would realize the unhealthiness of my attachment to Helen.

My connections with women have always been more profoundly complicated than my relationships with men. I usually knew where I stood with a man: either they were interested or not. There was often lightness to our repartee that lacked the mystery and complexity of that with many women. I frequently feel the need to be cautious with females, not to appear too needy or grasping, but often I don't succeed. I am scared around women—undoubtedly looking for unconditional mother love and a sense of identity. Nothing new in that revelation, I venture, but it's one that must be repeatedly looked at to move on to adulthood.

Following a time of terrifying introspection (I often considered suicide) and the usual therapy, I have joined a twelve-step program that I drag my ass to daily. I was surprised that no one tried to dissuade me by claiming that I did not need it. My drug use was no longer a joke as I ended up in the hospital after smoking grass and cigarettes in the freezing cold—my lungs almost shutting down.

I understand that when Helen heard I was hospitalized for pneumonia, she claimed that I deserved it. She said it was due to my lifestyle. She was not wrong. Toxicity comes in all forms, both chemical and organic. If I choose to grow up, I might learn to avoid both. I might even develop a couple of healthy relationships with women—sober and clear-headed, where I don't sacrifice my self-worth in an attempt to reappear as something else.

A lifelong New Yorker, Melody Breyer-Grell was a voracious reader as a little girl, which led toward a life filled with theater, opera, and jazz. After studying opera at the Curtis Institute of Music, Melody's CD, The Right Time, won the prestigious Best Vocal CD of 2004 in New York City's All About Jazz magazine. She has written as a critic for Cabaret Scenes magazine. Publications include the Fairhaven Literary Review and The Cat's Meow for Writers and Readers Magazine, and her short stories have been featured in Counting Down the Seconds and SunKissed. With strong opinions about almost everything, Melody is a frequent contributor to the Huffington Post. She is working on her memoir, My Dog is Better Than Your Dog—Tails of Narcissism. You can listen to Melody at www.melodybreyer-grell.com and read her columns on www.cabaretscenes.com and www.huffingtonpost.com.

Ten Days

Suzanne Herman

There are two kinds of snowfalls. It used to snow here every winter. Whether a dusting or a storm there would always be flakes, gathering on doorposts and window ledges behind which people sat, warm and dry. But once the last storm broke, the largest the town had ever seen, it never fell again. It was like we had used up our allotment, like we'd been greedy and were being punished, like we'd spent it all on one last hurrah. It hasn't snowed here in over twenty years. But I was here when it did, and I still know about the snow. I know, for instance, that there are two kinds of snowfalls. There is the one that leaves the air gray and foggy, the other that leaves it sharp and refreshing to breathe. People in the first kind of snowstorm grow irritated; they stomp the water from their boots and shout over the noise and inconvenience of the snowplows. Families who try to venture out in that weather are soon driven away by ice and sludge and the layer of dirt that lies hidden beneath even the cleaned snow. The second type of snowstorm does not complicate the world. It is not an obstacle to overcome. Instead, things are laid bare. The slate is wiped clean of grime and replaced by pure, flat light, encompassing everything, silencing the noise and casting a hush over people and homes.

In first grade Lucy and I had cubbies next to each other at school. The colored paper that hung above my cutout in the back wall of the classroom was blue, hers red. Together, I told her proudly, we made purple.

For the first few years of our friendship I recognized no difference between Lucy and me. When we played make-believe under the slide at recess we imagined the same fantasies; when we spent sleepless nights giggling in each other's bedrooms we had the same questions and the same fears. To me our hair was not respectively blond and brown but jointly a dark gold. Similarly, our families were not headed by separate sets of parents but instead by four mighty powers telling us when to eat and when to stop running. Nothing fazed me about our relationship; its road stretched ahead far and uninterrupted.

The largest snowstorm in the history of the town where Lucy and I lived happened during our senior year of high school. The flakes started falling at nine in the morning. Neither teacher nor student during second period that day could keep from glancing out the window every few minutes, watching the cement of the sidewalks go from tan, to gray, to transparent under a dusting of ice, to a white that deepened before our eyes. We watched the windows fog and the trees grow shorter. If it continues like this, we thought, they'll have to shut down the whole town. By lunchtime school had been canceled for the next day. Students started to file out of the building, walking slowly with their faces turned upward toward the sky. We gathered at whichever house was closest; already cars and buses were afraid of being trapped by the growing heaps.

Lucy and I spent the first night of the storm with a few other girls in the basement of a friend's house. Not yet believing in the power of the storm we talked only about schoolwork and movies, unable to see or sense the shifting winds from our hideout in the basement's dark back room. When we woke up the next morning, the storm had completely taken over. Lucy and I stood at the doorstep of the house, overlooking a long expanse of street that led onto a park.

We exhaled.

The snow lay a foot and a half deep in every direction. Untouched by footprint or shovel it had elevated the street into one long white platform, stretching infinitely. Cars parked along the side of the road were now merely rounded metal roofs, not a wheel or hubcap in sight. The stairs at our feet, which usually sloped steeply to an iron gate, were now a slide of pure and unbroken snow. Not a thing stirred on the road or in its surrounding houses. I wondered for a moment if we weren't the only two people left, unfrozen, in the whole place.

Lucy and I were born ten days apart. We were born in the same room of the same hospital in the same town. Silly, really, I often thought, for those ten days to have separated us. It would have been cleaner, simpler, had we taken our first breaths together. The maternity ward we were born in must have felt slightly off the day I arrived, somehow off balance. The nurses were probably puzzled, having never delivered half a child before. When they handed me to my mother they must have smiled timidly, hoping she wouldn't notice that her bundle of joy was only a fraction of what it should be, so that they could go home on time to their own undivided children. Although Lucy and I didn't meet for another six years, I assume that all it took to steady the world was her being in it. Us being in the world together.

We walked to Lucy's house that first morning of the storm. In the past the familiar trip had taken minutes, but this time we lingered every few steps, rotating slowly with our eyes on the treetops. We walked in the middle of what any other day would have been the main line of traffic. The snowplows, they said, were stuck in their garages. The city was quiet as we walked, muffled under mounds of chill and fluff.

"Hello!" I shouted at the ground, now inseparable from the sky in shade or shape. Even our calls were drowned in the frozen expanse of the new planet. By the time we had trekked to Lucy's low-roofed house it felt as if this was how the world had always been. Colors were only variations of white and any sound only the echo of falling snow.

When I look back on it now, I realize how much magic there was in it. Those ten days in my calendar are as blank as the land was, like a large white block had been dropped in the path of my life. Like nature had handed down a great, snowy respite. When you were in it you could see neither forward nor backward, like flying through a cloud in an airplane. Despite everything going on in the world, with all the technology we possessed and the things we could accomplish, one gust of nature had brought it all to a halt. The snow made all else useless. Calm down, the white streets said to me then, and whisper faintly to me now. Stop for a while, and when you're ready you can start again.

On the third day of the storm Lucy and I sat at the base of the hill in the park and packed snowballs. We faced the brick wall of the nearest building, coated as it was in soft powder.

"College," I said and threw the snowball at the wall. It burst magnificently and fell to the ground like fine sand.

"Parents," Lucy said and sent her snowfall flying.

Expectations. Ambitions. Distance. Longing. Trust. We threw them all at the wall one by one, watching them shatter and turn into air. The strength of the words was palling before us. It was hard to acknowledge their existence in a place like this, seemingly void of complications. Disrespect, which I threw, and vanity, which Lucy threw, are jagged and complex sensations. Nothing that wasn't smooth or effortless existed here.

On the fifth day we climbed the hill, dotted now with figures in bulky black coats. We had no choice but to scale the steep incline by walking around abandoned sleds and lost mittens. We reached the summit out of breath, the fresh high-altitude air stinging with each gasp. We looked around in awe at the town we thought we knew, the one we had looked at our entire lives. The snow had erased the baseball diamond, the playground, the parking lot, the small man-made lake, the nearby streets and gardens. Every rise and fall of the land had been leveled by an immense blanket of frost. The entirety of existence was uniform whiteness, the dots of color floating below just the tops of people's knit caps. And here we were, standing above it all.

"It's amazing," I breathed.

"Incredible," she said back, neither of us looking away from the vast stretch of time and space before us. The magnificence of the moment, how much it meant to me and how striking it all was, these words were caught in the back of my stinging throat. It catches you off guard, a view like that, and makes you look for some kind of perspective. If the rest of your life, all added up, still isn't as breathtaking and as shocking as this view, you ask yourself, what does it say about that life? So we simply stayed silent.

From the multitude of possible problems that could have befallen Lucy and me during our years of school together, we chose—carefully, it seemed—to grow briefly apart when we were eleven years old. It was like an experiment, like throwing a boomerang to see if it will come back or pulling apart a piece of clay to see if you can put it back together again, unchanged. We talked with other girls, ate different pack lunches, memorized other people's phone numbers, and otherwise lived separate lives. As if we were two completely unconnected selves. But as the weather would have it, that summer was the one that our parents—now two distinct but friendly sets—sent us to the same camp in the north woods. One night during the first week Lucy swung herself down from the bunk above me and sat tentatively on the edge of my bed. She looked at me with watery eyes. One minute they were blue and the next they were muddied by my brown ones, just as I had imagined them in the early days of our friendship. The great experiment had ended. We held each other close and cried in one long stream. Every night after that one, Lucy would slide her hand down through the space between our bunk and the wall so that I could reach it by propping myself up on an elbow. We'd squeeze each other's hand tightly before drifting to sleep.

When Lucy and I were both fifteen, I just that much closer to sixteen than she, the popular game of the moment was played in pairs. It was a card game played by four people, each holding four cards. The extra cards in the deck were passed from person to person so that they could trade them for one in their own hand. When one eager participant got four of the same card all at once, they were supposed to signal secretly to their partner. The partner could then slap the table and with a triumphant yell win the round for their team. Lucy and I never lost a game. Tell us your signal, friends would say, hoping to employ our method. But the truth was that Lucy and I never bothered to think up a secret signal, a subtle shoulder gesture or flick of the hair, like our girlfriends did. When Lucy held four queens in her hand I could feel them weighing down my own. I assumed that she too felt light with the pleasure of imminent victory as soon as I had picked the last nine from the deck and held it, hidden, across from her. Cheaters, the other players would call us, abandoning Lucy and me for two less compatible opponents. Maybe we were cheating. After all, everybody else was playing with two people, and our team was only one.

How did we spend the seventh day of wind-rattled windows and snow-capped streetlamps? Only one memory, recalled as if through a pane of wintry glass, comes back to me. We couldn't have been there for more than two hours, but all I can remember from that day is Lucy and me lying in an especially large pile of snow in her front yard. Maybe the rest of the family was inside having a party, or eating dinner, or playing Scrabble.

I couldn't have told you even then. Lucy and I lay on our backs looking directly up at the sky. If it were possible I would say that we didn't blink the entire time, so intensely and constantly do I remember staring at the pale blue above, occasionally wiping flakes from my eyes, nose, and forehead. We were enveloped in silence and open space, wrapped tightly in it like a baby in swaddling clothes. Even if we had tried to talk, the few feet of distance between us, comprised as it was of solid snow, would have made it impossible.

However, now that I think of it, it could be that Lucy did try to speak to me as we lay there passing the hours. It's possible, I guess, that I didn't hear her. I wouldn't have been able to laugh at any jokes she told, and any questions would have gone unanswered.

I hear about Lucy now in my peripheral hearing. Her name comes at me in whispers from unseen corners, from the far end of dinner-party tables. When I least expect it I'm startled by questions that begin "What ever happened to . . . ?" Our shared community still exists, the one made up of mutual friends and family members who love to ask after long-forgotten classmates. But I haven't spoken to Lucy since the snow stopped falling. I've heard over the years the hallmarks of her life: how her thesis was received, how her car was stolen, how her husband proposed, how old her daughter was when she walked, how she spent the summer before college with a broken leg. I nod. I find myself thinking about her only when I see frost on windows. Whether it's from snow or mist or the afterimage of breath on glass I am transported to scenes, like snapshots, of Lucy. Lucy at summer camp, sun-soaked and laughing, Lucy asleep on the couch, Lucy in tears as a child, Lucy standing on a hill of snow. But when the mist dissolves, so do the pictures, and I'm left, quite comfortably, with myself. I am lighter now, carrying around only one self.

There is no friend like that first. There is no confidant or partner so dear. The first love learned, our first friend is our mother, our spouse, and our child. But once that second soul is gone, the need for it fades. Thoughts aren't communal anymore; desires are not spoken. And what of it? Much worse things have been left behind, much more of history has wilted and been forsaken. The lame cannot be carried along.

On day ten of the largest snowstorm in our town's history the sky turned golden. Every impossibility, every instance of splendor and amazement that had already taken place during that storm, the tenth day produced tenfold. If there was any light left to be gleaned from the snow on the ground, it chose to shine now. The flakes, nearly perfect in their spiral to earth as they had been, perfected themselves on that morning. The result was an atmosphere that vibrated with a glow. Every ice-covered surface acted as a mirror, turning the hill that Lucy and I summited for the second time into an almost celestial beacon.

On the hill on what was clearly the last of our snow days—the icicles on rooftops were beginning to drip, the white sidewalks were melting and pouring pure water into the sewer grates, and the snowplows were said to have been freed from their garage prisons—Lucy and I reminisced. The enigmatic ban on speech that the snow had laid dissolved as the ice did. We listed what we had done over those past ten days, convincing ourselves that it had all really happened. The walk from school, we said, the hill, the metaphoric snowballs, the views, the air, and the streets. We were elated, we said, reflective, passionate, and unwound. It was a slow but obvious descent from here into every moment shared between us, every moment we had both lived. Needless to say this took some hours, the listing and considering of those innumerable moments that in total shaped a life we had practically lived together. One entity, looking back on its own existence with two perspectives, trying to procure new information, to give the time spent more significance.

We sat cross-legged in the snow, or as close to cross-legged as we could get in our thick snow pants and heavy boots. We sat for so long that we lost our legs in the rising snow. Eventually we lost our hands, too, resting flat on the ground to support us, in the slowly falling flakes. So when we rose at last it was with a sense of creation and birth, the parts of ourselves we had so recently lost appearing good as new before. We stood at the hill's edge, at its steepest point, the slope downward coated so heavily in ice that it gave the appearance of a long glass slide stretching to a line of dark trees at its base. From looking out again at the view Lucy and I turned to smile broadly at each other.

Then Lucy fell. As she reeled forward she stretched out her arm, well within my reach to catch and steady her, but instead I jumped away as if frightened. So sudden was the disturbing sensation that gripped me that I leaped from Lucy in terror. *I ought to be falling too.* Farther back now on the hilltop I couldn't see Lucy as she fell, I assume, in a splayed and graceless fashion toward the bottom. From where I stood, immobile, I could hear faint crunching noises, like bones breaking or like a child stepping on dry leaves. At last I heard a thump, like someone rolling into a clump of dark trees or like kicking a soccer ball. Either way, what I heard next was certainly, definitively, a deafening silence. It was accompanied by still air.

It's easy to start over if life has recently begun again. If the storm has lifted and everyone is stepping from their houses to line the streets with curious, full, rejuvenated faces—and shovels—then no one asks any questions. They have all just now emerged, slate clean, round two.

I stood rooted to my spot, seconds passing as I gazed at the melting world before me. When I felt secure on the ground, positive that I would not fall, I turned and carefully climbed down the hill on its opposite side. From there I walked home, as children who have not quite developed that mortal knowledge of consequence might do, alone.

Suzanne Herman is a student at Barnard College in New York City. She is currently pursuing a Bachelor's Degree in English Literature with a concentration in Creative Writing. When not studying in NYC she can be found reading and writing in her hometown of Chicago.

Part Four:
Women Remember

Striving for balance.

How I Lost Her

Ann Hood

We talked. In whispers during class. Behind closed bedroom doors on the telephone. On double dates. At the mall as we picked out new 45s, lip gloss, miniskirts. Over ice cream sundaes, cheeseburgers, onion rings. During movies. Over tarot cards and Ouija boards. In home ec. At play rehearsals, during study hall, in the library. Lying on the beach, body-surfing, climbing rocks. Riding in cars and on buses and trains and planes. In London, Manhattan, Honolulu, Rio de Janeiro. While we drank wine and beer and good strong coffee. At parties. At bars. At the junior prom. At my wedding. At her wedding. Breastfeeding. Looking at Monet, Matisse, Degas paintings. In bookstores. In her apartment. In my apartment. Long distance. Late at night. On our cell phones. For thirty-five years we talked. And then we were silent.

I did not believe my life would be defined by tragedy even though trag-edy always hovered at its borders. An aunt dead at age twenty-three during surgery to remove her wisdom teeth. A grandfather dying young from a mosquito infected with equine encephalitis on a trip to Block Island. An uncle dropping dead at thirty-five while he danced with his wife on Valentine's Day.

These stories, these tragedies, made my grandmother wail and pull her hair and carry huge pots of geraniums, poinsettias, chrysanthemums to cemeteries across Rhode Island. They made my mother sad, marking her losses by sleeping all day, crying at night, staring off in the distance as if she might actually find her sister or brother or father there.

Our family had had its share. That's what I believed. Those dead people, those sad stories, seemed far away from my life in 1968. That's when I met Amelia. Seventh grade. Mrs. Junker's math class. New math. I didn't like it, the math. I wrote haikus in the margins. I daydreamed about meeting Dino Danelli, the drummer for the Young Rascals. I had found his name in a Manhattan telephone book in the basement of the town library, and I saved my dimes until I had enough to call him from a pay phone, also in the library basement. I called him and listened to him saying, "Who is this? Hello?" Then I hung up and saved more dimes.

While Mrs. Junker wrote equations on the board, Amelia took careful notes. She furrowed her brow. She erased and rewrote and tried harder. I wrote down the words to "Sounds of Silence" from memory. No one understood new math. Not even Steven Smeal, the math whiz.

Then one day, Amelia's face brightened while Mrs. Junker explained something. Amelia nodded. She understood new math! I watched her understanding and I was impressed. Amelia had black hair already turning gray. Also impressive for a twelve-year-old. She had big, round brown eyes and still wore handmade dresses. I wore black armbands to protest the Vietnam War and could almost sit on my long dirty blond hair. I had just acquired a pair of round wire-rimmed glasses, like John Lennon's.

But I leaned over and whispered, "Show me how to do it." She didn't want to get in trouble, but she explained, nervously glancing up to be sure Mrs. Junker wasn't looking at us. After class I asked her for her phone number: 821-1952. I asked her to go to the mall on Saturday. She wasn't sure her father would let her. We walked to class together. That is how I found her.

But this is how I lost her.

Thirty-five years later. We are finally living in the same state again, Rhode Island. She never left it. I never wanted to come back. But I did. She was married and had a daughter and lived about as far away from me as two people in such a small state can. I was married and had a son and a daughter. It was hard to get Amelia out with me. I called her every week. We tried to make plans. Sometimes we actually saw each other.

This week, mid-April 2002, her husband was going away. My husband was going away. We got babysitters. Chose a movie and a restaurant. Girls' night out. Then, my five-year-old daughter, Grace, spiked a 105-degree fever and died thirty-six hours later from a virulent form of strep. Friends started arriving at my house, where I sat numb and horrified at what had happened, at what we had lost. "Call Amelia," I told someone. And someone did.

I said I did not think my life would be one marked by tragedy. But it is. In 1982, when I was working as a flight attendant, I went out for Mexican food in L.A. with the crew on a layover. As I walked down the hall toward my hotel room, I heard the telephone ringing. And in that way that we know somehow there is bad news on the line, I did not want to answer that phone. But it kept ringing, as I turned my key in the lock, and walked inside, and kicked off my shoes, it would not stop. It was 9:00 p.m., midnight on the East Coast. Finally, I picked it up. A man I had just broken up with said, "I have bad news," and I hung up on him and started to cry before I even knew what he was going to tell me; there was disaster in his voice. He called back and I hung up again. But the third time he told me not to hang up. "There's been an accident and your brother is dead. There's an eleven o'clock flight to Boston and you have to take it. You have to get home." I wrote down the flight information on the hotel pad by the phone. Then I told him, "Call Amelia."

I don't remember that flight. But I remember walking out of Logan Airport into the early morning light of the first day of July, and seeing Amelia waiting there for me in her Subaru. Amelia always bought reliable cars, things that lasted. She was sensible and steadfast. She had a retirement fund. She clipped coupons.

That day she drove me the hour to my parents' house, and although I don't remember them exactly, she said all the right things. When we got there, she walked me inside and waited until I told her it was okay to go. For the rest of that summer, as I watched my mother unravel and my father struggle and my brother's seven-year-old daughter's confused face, Amelia brought me beers and sat in the heat of the long nights with me, drinking them.

When I moved to New York City a few months later, I tried to take her with me. But Amelia was firmly footed in Rhode Island. She did not like change. I went off to do the exploring for both of us. And frequently she came to stay with me in my tiny apartments. I would draw her maps of the subway with careful notes on where to get off. I would point her toward Canal Jeans and the good magazine store. Then we would have Chinese food delivered and eat it with cheap wine and talk about love and sex. We would giggle just like we did when we were twelve and wondered what love and sex were all about. With a best friend, an old friend, one word can send you into fits of laughter. Plums! Wood chips! Zinfandel! We would whisper

these to each other in bed, and laugh, and keep talking until talk turned to
sleep unnoticed.

In this time of most enormous grief after Grace died, there is no day or
night. There is just loss. People put food on a plate and hand it to you to
eat. They fill your glass with good strong scotch. They arrive at your house
with shopping bags filled with Kleenex, new tablecloths, salads. Things you
don't even know you need because the only thing you really need—your
daughter's hug, her sleepy body curled into your lap, her voice calling out to
you—is gone and will never come back. You can't sleep; you can only sleep.
You cry. You scream. You look for her in the corners of each room, search
the pockets of her backpack for something left behind, lift her coat to your
nose to find her smell, hold her brush to the light to marvel at her pale
blond hair still tangled there. A week passes. A month. It grows hot and
then cold and then hot again. Friends take your son to school, pack him
a lunch, keep him for hours while you sit in your bed and cry. Friends go
over and over and over with you those thirty-six hours that have changed
your life. They bring you coffee and ginger scones. They drive from New
York City just to hold your hand for a few hours. They climb into bed with
you and hug you. They water the plants that keep arriving, and make fun
of the bad ones because they know you have a wicked sense of humor. They
send their own children with babysitters so they can sit with you and watch
Mario Batali make pudding out of bologna and pizza topped with pork fat.
They take you for walks. They take you to the movies. They do your laundry. And time is somehow passing, unbelievably. The world keeps moving
even without Grace in it.

But among these faces, this endless flow of friends who never let you
be alone because that is the worst thing of all, Amelia's is absent. A note
came through the mail slot, delivered by hand. It did not say anything different than all the other notes that arrived those first days expressing love
and sadness. A glimpse of her at the memorial service where hundreds of
people filled the church while my son sang "Eight Days a Week" for his
sister. But in the crush of hugs and tears afterward, I could not find her
face.

Then it happens. I find myself alone one morning. There are so many
people I can call. I know that. But it is her number I dial. When I hear
her voice, I start to cry. I say her name. My loss is still new, a few weeks at
most. "Can you come?" I ask her. I can hear the desperation in my voice.

She is at work. She hesitates. She tosses out reasons why she cannot come right this minute. A mammogram appointment. Her daughter needs a ride somewhere. I can't keep talking because panic is rising in my throat. The panic of grief, of being alone with it. My house has become a minefield. Grace's glittery nail polish, the MOM she shaped into a crown out of pipe cleaners, the shoehorn she used dramatically to put on her sneakers, her ballet tights tossed under the bed.

I can't go out there alone, I want to say Amelia. But I am having trouble forming words, except the most basic ones: Why? Help. Grace. Amelia says she will come another day. Her voice is appropriately somber. "Okay," I say. "Tomorrow?" I am desperate. All I can see ahead are hours and days like the ones I am having. "Not tomorrow. But soon. I'll call you."

And she never did. Almost two years have passed and I have never seen her again. That day I called another friend, and she came. They kept on coming, my friends. They still do. But Amelia is gone.

I have lost her before.

In ninth grade, I was smitten with a different friend. She wore halter tops and French-kissed boys and spent the afternoons alone while her parents worked, making cookies and calling boys and doing the Ouija board. When my mother let me choose a friend to come to the beach, I chose Marie and broke Amelia's heart. She never let me forget it, the wound never healed. Years later she would remind me of that summer when I spent my days with Marie instead of her.

But by September—tenth grade! High school finally! It was Amelia and I again. We auditioned for *Fiddler on the Roof* and spent every afternoon in the high school auditorium singing "Anatevka" and "Matchmaker." We got boyfriends by asking them to the school's Sadie Hawkins dance, our first official double date. The boys were neighbors and best friends, and every Saturday night the four of us went to the movies and then for strawberry pie or steak sandwiches before parking by the golf course and kissing until our curfews.

We went to different colleges. She stayed put and I kept moving away. She had real jobs where she had to be Monday through Friday, all day. I drifted and drifted. But when we came together, there were no differences. We took trips together, always agreeing on where to go and what to do there. We saw plays and movies and went to museums. Our talk about these things was endless.

Other people saw only our differences. Our lives kept moving away from each other, and to outsiders it was hard to see what kept our friendship going. Our husbands had nothing in common. Our kids' ages were far apart. Our tastes in superficial things—houses, cocktails, pets—were completely different. And larger issues—our futures, our dreams—diverged as well. Our teenage selves had fantasized about becoming a painter (Amelia) and a writer (me). The world had seemed both vast and small enough for us to hold in our hands. But our adult selves did not want the same romantic things. One day Amelia told me that when her daughter went to college, she wanted to sell her house and move into a trailer in the woods. I laughed until I saw she meant it. How had she arrived there? I wondered.

But still we met somewhere rooted in history and girlish dreams. When a newer friend asked me one night why I still stayed friends with Amelia—"You two have nothing in common!"—I got angry. Amelia, I told her, was my best friend, and always would be. We could still sing all the words to "Matchmaker" and resurrect our own version of "Tiny Bubbles"; we could sit together after a Chagall show and talk for hours about what we'd just seen. She'd held my hand after my brother died. We'd helped each other through the death of each of our fathers. How dare anyone question us, Amelia and me?

The last time I saw Amelia—not the glimpse of her through my tears at Grace's memorial service, but really saw her—was Oscar night 2002. Amelia and I watched the Oscars together whenever we could. We discussed who would be nominated, called each other after the nominations were announced, went together to see as many movies as we could before the big night.

Sometimes I gave elaborate Oscar parties, with trivia games and prizes and costumes. But this year, I invited only a small group of people and made dinner to eat while the stars walked down the red carpet. Amelia arrived with a small Oscar statue. "You can take it out every year on Oscar night," she said. We debated whether to use it as a prize if we played a game or to keep it as the one standard for our own Academy Awards.

Grace wanted to go to bed early that night. So she crawled into a sleeping bag and went to sleep right by the television. I remember Amelia saying good night to Grace before she left for her hour's ride back home. She didn't wait to hear who won Best Movie. She was worried about the time, and the long drive. "Good night, Grace," she said, and she was gone.

"Why don't you call her?" my husband asks me when I tell him Amelia has left me for good.

He doesn't understand the complexities of women's friendships, how hurts sometimes cannot be forgotten, or forgiven. How three decades later, Amelia could still get teary remembering the summer I spent with Marie instead of her. It is the ultimate betrayal to abandon your good friend—for a man, for another woman, or when she needs you desperately.

"What would I say if I called her?" I ask my husband, and my throat burns even thinking of her voice on the other end of the telephone.

"Say whatever you want," he says, shaking his head.

But all I want is to know how she could have left me. I am confused and angry and hurt.

"Perhaps losing Grace scared her," a friend told me. "If it can happen to you, it can happen to her."

It is true that some people bend their heads when I pass by, as if what has happened is contagious. It is true that there are not the right words to say. A breezy "How are you doing?" can make me angry because the answer is I'm terrible, I'm paralyzed, I'm broken.

I am told that some people don't know what to do, what to say, how to approach me. Is it possible that Amelia is among those women who avoid me because it's easier? Or because they are incompetent in the face of tragedy? She was always someone who held back emotionally. When her father died, I couldn't get her to talk about it. She'd hang up quickly, her voice muffled. One day I demanded she tell me just how bad she felt, and she did, forcefully. But only that once.

I was the friend who called more, who got tickets to a play or made a point of seeing movies together. She would go months without talking to friends of hers, I know that. Sometimes circumstances overwhelmed her, like too much work or parenting or simply a difficult week. Still, I believed that I—we—were immune to that. Distance, lifestyles, careers, none of it had kept us apart before.

In my grief, casual friends have become good friends; good friends have become family. Women keep surprising me. The mother from my son's school, the one I hardly know, sends me a card every month. A woman who I met just a few weeks before Grace died didn't retreat but instead emerged with humor and strength to become one of my dearest friends.

But my best friend, my oldest friend has left me, as easily as we found each other over a confusing equation thirty-five years ago.

My son, Sam, is a member of an all-children's theater ensemble. One night, after a play, he came up to me, excited and confused.

"You'll never guess who was here," he said. "Amelia and her daughter."

I looked around the crowded lobby.

"No, they left," he said. "I saw them in the audience and then afterward I came out to say hello, and I saw them walking out."

"Did she talk to you?" I asked him. My heart pounded as if an old lover had shown up.

Sam shook his head. He described her in great detail, and her daughter, who looked older now, he said, and wore glasses. He led me to the book where people signed up to be on the mailing list, and there was her name, in a penmanship I know as well as my own.

Had she seen me? I wondered. Surely she had recognized Sam's name in the program. Had she left to avoid me? To avoid us?

Before Grace died, I always invited her to Sam's plays—*Oliver!* and *Stuart Little* and *A Midsummer Night's Dream*. But she could never make it. Now she shows up at every one of Sam's plays. But she does not stay long enough to say hello.

I wonder what I would say if I cornered her one night, if I could even find the words to express what I have endured these two long years without her. She held my hand senior year in high school when an older boy, a college boy, broke my heart. She sat next to me at my father's funeral. She kneeled beside me when I threw up in the snow after too many kamikaze shots. I wonder if she would tell me why she deserted me now, when I needed her more than ever. As time passes, it gets harder to believe that I will let her back into my life and harder to believe she would try.

She does not slip a note through our door, or call to see how we are faring, this wobbly three-person family of mine. I wonder if she remembers the night we took Sam and her daughter to see *The Fantasticks* at the little theater on Sullivan Street, and how during intermission Sam got on the stage and reenacted the Man Who Would Not Die. "He's going to be onstage someday," she said, in the wise voice she sometimes used. "I just know it." Does she remember that I cried that night when they sang "Try to remember the kind of September, when life was slow, and oh, so mellow . . ."? She teased me for crying, but I always was the sentimental one. Does she remember why we used to laugh when one of us said "Plums!" or "Wood chips!" or "Zinfandel!"? Or is all of it, all the thread of our friendship, lost too?

My husband brings home the list of names of people who sent in donations to the scholarship fund we started in Grace's name. He points to one, and I look down and see Amelia's name and a generous contribution. So she is out there, she is thinking of me. But she remains silent, as if in this, there is nothing, nothing, she can say. Her silence is loud, it breaks my heart.

Ann Hood is the author of the best-selling novels The Knitting Circle, The Red Thread, *and* Somewhere Off the Coast of Maine. *Her memoir,* Comfort: A Journey Through Grief, *was a New York Times Editors' Choice and was chosen as one of the top ten nonfiction books of 2008 by* Entertainment Weekly. *Hood has been the winner of two Pushcart Prizes and Best American Spiritual, Travel, and Food Writing awards. Her most recent novel is* The Italian Wife *and she edited* Knitting Yarns: Writers on Knitting *in 2014. Hood lives in Rhode Island.*

Never Can Say Good-bye

Jessica Handler

When I was very young, my father worked peripherally in politics. From watching him, I learned to be outgoing, to always smile and shake hands, to remember names. I actually curtsied once, caught in a fit of panic about the most respectful way to greet the widow of a slain civil rights leader. Politics was great training. I remember names; I'm outgoing; I always smile and shake hands.

Which is probably why I've never officially "dumped" a friend. As a grown woman, I can easily extricate myself from the early stages of a friendship before it develops a toxic sheen. This is dumping before actual dumping. Let's call it a careful redeployment of my assets.

I've been overtly dumped only once. I was "unfriended." This befuddles me more for the timidity of merely changing a computer setting to define if a friendship is "off" or "on" than for the loss of the friendship itself. I'd like to think that were I to "unfriend," I would do so with a human touch. I'd stop calling. I'd create reasons why I couldn't meet for lunch or attend *shayna punim*'s bat mitzvah. (The excuse "I'd rather clean the bathtub with my tongue" truly does beg for a polite white lie.)

I cherish the very good friends I've made as an adult. Adult friends will eat an entire wheel of Camembert with you at one sitting, teach you to fly a kite because you never learned, and tell you, not so delicately, when you're not living up to your potential. Adult friends bring the good bourbon. Some of my strongest adult friendships subtly acknowledge those childhood too-much-of-a-loser-to-be-picked-for-Red Rover years, but our not having been on the playground together makes all the difference. We're not responsible for each other's misery. When a friend grouses to me that everyone but her at a high-toned reception was a "cool kid," there's no explanation necessary. Like bats in the dark, we're responding to each other's sonar.

My childhood friends are the ones I can't dump, although from the vantage point of this writing, a few appear highly dumpable. These women aren't exactly "frenemies"—they're not friends, per se, but neither have they descended so far on the ex-friend spectrum to become actual enemies. I can't disentangle myself from the woman who's taken to praying for me via digital greeting card, or the woman who went from being a bossy ten-year-old to a bossy fifty-year-old. (We lost touch in the intervening years, and now that we've reconnected, I'm tempted to throw a tantrum and scream, "You're not the boss of me!")

It's up to me, as the friend who can't dump anyone, to take the prayer e-mails, the unsolicited and meddlesome advice, and, for that matter, the signing of the birth announcement with an autopen, in the spirit in which they were given. These people were bound to grow up this way. And I was bound to grow up to be the woman who could never quite turn out the light and leave them in the dark.

These friends from childhood and my young adulthood are the other halves of my memory. If no one but me remembers that the pig in our seventh-grade classroom was named Willadene (or even that there was a sow in our city school in the first place), it's possible that there *was* no pig. If I alone recount the tale of the night in college when my friends and I walked across the glassy, frozen Charles River from Boston to Cambridge, did we actually do it?

Siblings are traditionally the avatars of collective memory, but by the time I was thirty-two, my two sisters had died. Susie died when she was eight. I was ten; Sarah was four. Sarah died at twenty-seven. I was a few months shy of thirty-three.

Without them in my life, much of my formative memory is a one-way mirror. I can tell you a little bit about the time Mom, Sarah, me, and a tabby kitten escaped my dad's rages for a mountain weekend, but the other half of that story will always be missing. Or the night the babysitter marched us around the yard armed with kitchen knives to battle her imaginary intruders? That's all mine now.

My adult friends came into my life after my sisters died, which affords our friendships a kind of freedom. We know what it was like to be a kid, but they didn't know me as a kid. They didn't know my sisters.

If I were the kind of woman to play fast and loose with the word *sister*, I could list a dozen friends, men and women, close enough and loved enough by me to merit that honorary title. But I'm jealous with the word. If my sisters don't get to apply the description to themselves, no one does.

I wonder if my sisters and I would have dumped one another somewhere along the line. I know that just because people have the same parents doesn't mean they'll get along. I like to think, though, that my sisters and I would have considered one another undumpable: that we'd have stayed a valiant trio. On the other hand, we might have grown to hold one another at a kind of psychic arm's length, the way you do with a friend who pushes all your buttons but you love too much to turn your back on entirely. You simply grit your teeth and bitch and wait for someone—certainly her, never you—to come to her senses.

I'll never be the one to tell a friend she's got to go. I'm pretty sure that if she does, a part of me will go with her.

Jessica Handler is the author of Braving the Fire: A Guide to Writing About Grief and Loss *(St. Martin's Press, December 2013). Her first book,* Invisible Sisters: A Memoir *(Public Affairs, 2009) was named one of the 2010 "Books All Georgians Should Read" by the Georgia Center for the Book. Her nonfiction has appeared on NPR and in* Tin House, Drunken Boat, Brevity, Newsweek, the Washington Post, *and* More *magazine. Honors include residencies at the Josef and Anni Albers Foundation, a 2010 Emerging Writer Fellowship from the Writer's Center, the 2009 Peter Taylor Nonfiction Fellowship, and special mention for a 2008 Pushcart Prize. Featured as one of nine contemporary Southern women writers in* Vanity Fair *magazine, she learned to never again wear couture. Find her at www.jessicahandler.com.*

Since I Don't Have You

Jacquelyn Mitchard

When she dumped me, there were times when I thought I would lose my reason.

Days melted as I wrote letters to her and destroyed them, cried until my lashes were spiked with salt, went out for a cup of coffee and got lost five miles from my own house. What was she doing, I thought, without me? Was she at a party with friends we both knew, exchanging the looks we once exchanged, across the clink and banter of an elegant crowd, but with someone else?

For nearly eighteen years we two had been one—what Carson McCullers once called "the we of me."

We were never lovers.

We were friends.

Yet our friendship was as powerful as any love affair.

So losing her was, I believe, as crushing as a divorce, and harder to repair in midlife than a divorce, or perhaps even a death in the family.

Your marriage ends; someone dies. It's horrific. It's unbearable. And yet, quickly, a circle of compassion surrounds you. People offer condolences, companionship, and casseroles.

You lose a friend and, unless you tell, no one even knows. If you do tell, no one much cares. Not even other women, who know that the loss of a friend is very different for a woman than it is for a man, that it's a crushing, terrifying experience—yet they say she was "just a friend." If you're part of a circle, it's foolish—and just wrong—to ask anyone to choose sides. Crying on the shoulder of another dear friend is asking that person to think, *What am I, chopped liver?* What do you say? "We had a fight"? Oh, it will blow over, people assure you.

"It seems impossible for such an epic friendship to go down over some ill-chosen words," said my pal Sam. "Give it time."

Now, I've given it time.

More than a year.

I've apologized for my part in the quarrel, passionately and more than once. She has sent her love and regret, hollow as a greeting card. How I felt at first, and how I still feel sometimes, is that I've lost a self, that I'm incomplete, no longer special.

Some friendships die a natural death. We change jobs. We move. The children who glue us to each other through social rites of passage grow up. Into those vacant spaces move new work buddies, new neighbors, and new members of the book club. And then, somehow, life becomes both slower and faster. You turn forty or fifty or sixty, and while you may be at the height of your earning power and your social influence, while you may be busier than you ever were before or will be again, the streams leaping with potential intimates—on the soccer sidelines, in college classes, and in new jobs—have simply dried up. Everyone else, for better or worse, already has her friendship cadre. There simply isn't the time to raise a friendship from a seedling to a mighty oak. Unless you are very lucky or persistent, getting to know anyone that intimately, without that shared history, from scratch, may now be impossible.

Some friendships die by negligent homicide.

We'd had only two other tiffs, in all those years—one silly, one a little more serious, both quickly mended. This was different. Liz has three sons, the youngest a loud-mouthed neohippie who thinks that anyone who's successful has sold her soul. A year ago, in public, he got in my face and finally said that if success were measured by looks, mine would be in the negative digits. I should have said nothing. I should have asked Liz to speak to him. But I didn't. I snapped and later privately wrote Anthony a note, reminding him that in high school he'd had a nose job.

That was the beginning of the end.

I remember the beginning. The first time I saw her was in the lobby of a theater in Chicago, greeting the audience after her heartbreaking portrayal of Thelma in Marsha Norman's 'Night, Mother. An actor, she was at work on writing her first full-length screenplay. By happenstance, we would end up, just months later, working at the same artists' residence. The chemistry was immediate. In the time it takes to brew a pot of coffee, we'd told each other things we'd never told another soul. And oh, how we laughed.

The Lady Elizabeth, my husband would call her, with just the slightest zest of envy, as I went on and on about something that Liz had quoted or worn or cooked to absolute perfection. Despite our manifest differences in temperature (she was lime sorbet and I was, perhaps, wasabi) we intersected at so many more places than most friends do, since I wrote books and essays and much that I did also pertained to playwriting.

We were both the happiest we'd ever been, at home even out of our natural habitat, like when one is swimming underwater. She once told me a story about one of her sons that made me laugh so hard I had to drive off onto a country road and pee in the bushes. I sent her lavender when her screenplay was optioned. She brought me chocolate when the IVF failed.

After our falling-out, it would be days before I realized that Liz was refusing my calls.

I thought she was just busy, or traveling with her husband, Charles, a landscape architect who'd cut his practice in half a few years ago. Liz had never let a day go by without returning my call.

When two days turned into three and then five, I couldn't believe it. Was she actually mad at me for bringing up the surgery Anthony had had to straighten his nose and give him a perfectly patrician profile? I'm sure Anthony didn't tell everyone he knew, but it was no big secret.

Lizzie mine, I wanted to cry, is this fair? Her son wasn't a high-school boy; he was twenty-seven. And *he* was the one who'd brought up appearances!

After an earlier misunderstanding, Liz and I had vowed total honesty in our relationship, swearing that if either of us was ever angry, we'd talk it out, then and there. Instead, Liz wrote me a letter, which took another week to arrive. By then, I was too hurt and outraged to open it. Instead, furious that she would drop me over what seemed a trifle, I fired off the lowest form of human communication, the excoriating e-mail, accusing Liz of being stingy emotionally and stingy in fact—reminding her that when we invited her and her husband for dinner, we served steak and Brie; they served soup and salad when we went over there. I gave her a luxurious shawl for Christmas; she gave me a mug.

Has there ever been a time in your life when you know you're wrong, then you realize you may be seriously wrong, but you're in so deep you can't stop and you keep blundering on, hoping you'll stumble over a justification?

It was like that.

Slowly, it came to me that I'd crossed a line in reprimanding her son. Even though he had insulted me, Liz's maternal feelings would never permit her to take my side. Still, she owed me some loyalty. I recanted, quickly sending a handwritten note wishing her well and pointing out that no more needed to be said. In truth, I wanted this episode to die a quick death with no postmortem. I didn't want to hear what I suspected was a litany of my failings. I never read her letter.

And then, there was nothing. Her silence was loud, and I knew that it meant the friendship was over.

Had I kept my temper, I might have kept her also.

Or maybe, I thought later, maybe not.

There was a ritual to go through: the process of dismantling our friendship.

A couples' vacation had to be canceled; substitutions were made for a seminar in which both of us were to teach; friends had to be alerted lest they invite us to the same dinner party. What I felt replacing my grief was terror. A woman without at least a few come-rain-or-come-shine friends is a woman on an ice floe, drifting. Two years before, in December, one of my scant handful of extraordinary friends, a woman I'd known for more than twenty years, had fallen into a coma when she contracted a rare form of strep. She would never awaken. My oldest and perhaps dearest friend was disabled by a chronic illness. This didn't make her any less beloved, but our contact was often by phone these days. What we could do together was limited. My fourth and perhaps closest friend (now) was much younger, in the throes of making babies. I happened upon an advice columnist named Marla Paul who, after going through an experience similar to mine, had written a book called *The Friendship Crisis: Finding, Making, and Keeping Friends When You're Not a Kid Anymore.* "It's so awkward," I recall reading. "You can't come on too strong, or the person will back away. But you have to put yourself out there. We have to remember that most people do want friends. Most people are delighted to meet for lunch." [6]

That was the last thing I felt able to do.

Instead, I could think only of the bounty of memories Liz and I shared, the ways in which time had intertwined our families and our other friends.

How could all that trust and laughter, touch and comfort and encouragement, be gone in the work of a moment? After the rift, I stopped using the phrases that had been ours. A Thai waiter had once told Liz, "There are three kinds of people. Number one kind of people? Want to die, can't." And that was the message we would leave for each other when times were hard: *Feeling like number one kind of people.*

I felt like number one kind of people. Missing her was nearly an ache, proving again to me that most of what we know as emotion is rooted in the physical.

Oddly, it was Liz who unknowingly started me back on the path to life without her. A note arrived from an acquaintance: *Saw Elizabeth at the gala, dancing the night away. I asked about you and she said she hadn't seen you lately. Where have you been hiding? I talked Elizabeth into joining our running club. What are you doing for fun?*

What was I doing for fun?

Drowning my sorrows in Bugles and onion dip?

I made a big decision. This was a big loss. I decided to visit a therapist.

In our three meetings, she helped me see deeper into my own grief, to ask myself why I was having so much trouble adjusting to life without this one person. I did have other dear friends, old and newer, whom I had all but neglected in giving so much of myself, the very best strawberries of my personal life, to Liz. Wisely, however, Liz had made sure to maintain close ties with her other friends—twice a month, she drove for two hours to meet another playwright named Asia for breakfast.

Did that hurt, the therapist asked? Yes, I said, quickly adding that Liz and I had had our own traditions. Do you think Liz would have gone so far for you, she asked? In fact, I'd quizzed Liz about that very thing, and her answer had been curious: She'd asked me why it mattered so much. And although when I mentioned a new person I'd met, Liz sometimes said things to me like "Do I have anything to worry about?" (this touched me deeply), she always meant it as a joke. For me, it was serious. I thought that someone more glamorous and secure, someone like Asia, would take Liz away from me. What it boiled down to was that I was only one of the elements that made Liz's life happy. And while the same was true for me, Liz took up a whole lot more real estate in my heart.

In therapy, I confronted some hard suspicions—about myself. With my other friends, was I most often the one who made the call, or the one who returned it? As we exchanged news, did I listen first, and listen well, no matter how much my own update quivered on the tip of my tongue? Was I the one to postpone the coffee date because my life was too busy? Not always, but too often, the answers were uncomfortable.

I wasn't being the friend I wanted to have.

And really, neither was Liz.

Admitting this was like losing her all over again. Still, it's the fact. One of the essentials of any great friendship is the ability to idealize the cherished one, to overlook most of her flaws, to shrug off most of her idiosyncrasies, unless they're genuinely toxic. For Liz, I had done that. I'd overlooked inflexibility and stubbornness, and the tiniest tendency to save her best china, literally and figuratively, for people she wanted to impress more. She had not been so understanding with me. Two bursts of temper and a bout of tears, earnestly repented, should not tip the scales of a friendship marked by so many joys.

There was also the matter of balance. Even factoring in Liz's need for tranquility (six times a month she spends a day in prayer and meditation, not even answering the phone), I always believed that a portion of Liz's time was enough for me. But it wasn't . . . not really. I do know that friendships aren't always truly mutual. In some, one person offers the kiss; the other offers the cheek. Most often I was the one who asked, and Liz the one who agreed. She only occasionally sought me out. That in itself didn't bother me very much. I'm no extrovert, and as an actor, Liz was always the center of a circle of admirers. That she wanted me at all made me feel worthy. But that prompted the question: Why did being without her make me feel not just sad, but like an outcast? Wasn't it her loss too?

How willing I was—and not just with Liz—first to lash out absurdly if I felt wronged, and then to feel overly culpable. Righteous indignation lasted for about a day, and then guilt took over. I now realized, however, that after a point, even if I had done the wrong thing—short of outright betrayal or actual harm—I had to stop beating myself up. It really does take two to end something. For Liz and me, there was blame to share. I should never have lost my temper and fired off that shameful tantrum. Still, nearly twenty years of supportive love and lyric memories deserved, if not lavish forgiveness, more than a letter.

This year has changed the landscape of friendship and me.

The cliché about being sadder but wiser is a cliché for a reason.

Of course I turned to my other friends, panicky, nearly ashamed of my need. I did not want to lose them. To my surprise, they welcomed me, happy to have more of my time. And I gave it, but with a difference.

Finding out how important I really *wasn't* to someone who meant the world to me made me examine why that was true.

I tend my friendships better now. I listen more and gently probe beneath the surface of things. More often, I remember the occasion or make the date, even though the timing might be less than convenient. Friendship isn't convenient. People don't know by telepathy that you care, and you can't keep them suspended in time until you're ready. So I make dates, rather than mere promises. At first, yes, I had to force myself. My link to Liz had made me smug; I always had the world's most charming pal in my back pocket. But although it might seem that doing something artificially makes it less than genuine, that's not the case. It's like regular exercise: at first you have to remind yourself; after a while it feels essential.

Several of the friendships I once considered second-tier are now filled with life and sentiment because I'm giving them the attention they always deserved. When something irks me, I still put it forcibly into context. I'll never be a pushover, but now I'm not so blunt. Before I hit the wall with an opinion, I'll try the detour. Now I literally honor the child's rule of counting to ten before I speak (and the cyber commandment of waiting overnight before I send an e-mail).

Inevitably, there came a day when I ran into Liz and Charles at a play. My three younger children, including my youngest, her godson, were with me. Liz stretched out her arms to him, but he was shy; it had been a year, and he didn't remember her.

"How are you, Jack?" Liz asked me. She looked truly concerned.

"I'm really okay," I told her, as bat wings of mascara, formed by my tears, gave lie to my words. "It's so good to see you."

It was good to see her. My heart had hungered for the hard hug of those fragile, graceful arms, for the luster of her smile. As the kids and I walked away, I glanced back. Liz had drawn down the brim of her straw hat and was leaning on Charles's shoulder. Perhaps there was a shadow in her life that still held my shape. I got into the car and adjusted the rearview mirror. In it I saw Liz throwing her arms wide and leaping with delight at the approach of her friend Asia.

Well. I would have wished it otherwise. I would have wanted to be the one who lit the light in her eyes. Still, I could be philosophical. It had taken half a century and a hard knock to teach me not to be more proud of having friends than of being one. Now, it's the other way around. Friendship for me is made from a tapestry of personalities, each of whom shares a part of all I care about.

As for Liz? There was only one.

I've welcomed new friends, and they mean more and more. I still trust. I still hope.

With just a little more time, I expect to be able to give my relationship with Liz the place it deserves in my life history. It's over. But it was, as Sam said, an epic friendship.

I fold it tenderly, as I would the baptismal gown of a child now grown. It is no longer useful. But it is still precious. It always will be mine.

Jacquelyn Mitchard is the author of numerous best-selling novels including The Deep End of the Ocean, *which was chosen as Oprah's first selection for her book club in 1996. The novel was made into a movie starring Michelle Pfeiffer. She is a longtime journalist, essayist, editor, writing instructor in several MFA programs, and mother of nine. Mitchard lives on Cape Cod. Find her at www.jacquelynmitchard.com.*

I Hate Your Boyfriend

Erin Eramia

The day I met the friend I will call Jenny, I was a twenty-five-year-old college graduate and had just ended an exhaustive job search by accepting a position as a grocery bagger. My boyfriend and I had been living with our friend Nicholas for a month or two when he brought her home. I came in from my first shift angry and discouraged. Jenny, a total stranger, sprang into action. I was leery of interrupting what seemed to be Nicholas's first date with what looked like an amazing girl, but she insisted I sit down.

"Are you a vegetarian?" she asked.

Why yes, yes I was.

"Here," she said, giving me a plate of lasagna and salad. We talked like old friends, and I soon forgot how miserable I was. Instead, I was thrilled. I knew I'd met my friendship soul mate.

Before she and Nicholas left, she noticed my improved mood. "See? No need to feel like crap about your stupid job. You won't be there long anyway." It was true.

Jenny and Nicholas didn't last, but Jenny and I did. We would sit at my kitchen table and talk for hours, still young and unencumbered enough to enjoy that luxury. We went to movies, went for walks, climbed trees. Jenny loved to dance, and loved all things tiny—tiny animals, tiny people, even what she called "tiny fiction." She was flirtatious with everyone she met in the most delightful and welcoming way. After work, she would often call me, saying, "I think what I need is a nice, stiff drink."

I once remarked that, in the grand scheme of things, maybe the purpose of her relationship with Nicholas had been to bring the two of us together. As soon as the words were out of my mouth, I regretted them. Jenny had loved Nicholas and been devastated by their breakup, and here I was trivializing it, making it all about me. Jenny wasn't offended. She was delighted with the idea and immediately latched onto it. We were kismet. After a rare argument, she said, "Well, this is the kind of thing that happens sometimes with lifelong friends. We're lifelong friends, right?" It sounded good to me.

One night, she and I went to a movie. It let out very late, and the streets were quiet and empty as I drove her home. But there was another car in front of us when we stopped at a red light. A couple sat in the front seats, clearly arguing. It seemed to escalate, and suddenly the driver punched the woman next to him in the side of the head, as swiftly as a snake striking its prey.

The light turned green. I didn't know what to do, so I attempted to follow them, asking Jenny to try to get their license plate number so we could call the police. I lost them within thirty seconds.

Jenny and I took deep breaths. I assumed Jenny, because she worked at Planned Parenthood and had strong feelings about domestic violence, felt as distraught as I did at having witnessed an act of violence and not been able to do anything.

"I mean, I didn't want to get us in a car accident following them, but maybe we could have done *something*?" I didn't have an answer, and Jenny looked at me like I'd lost my mind. She was not pleased that I'd dragged her along on my ten-second mission.

"When you see someone getting violent, you don't get *closer*," she said. It was a fair point, but the last thing I'd expected of her. I had grown up in a stable, middle-class home, whereas Jenny had grown up in brutality and poverty at the other end of the country. I had known that. We'd been friends for at least a year and had shared a lot of our past experiences. But the chasm between our worldviews had never seemed wider. In the car in front of us, I had witnessed someone else in danger. Jenny had been in danger herself. She didn't have the luxury of believing she could fix these things. If my response to violence was a complicated, ineffectual panic, hers was simple: Get. Me. Out. Of. Here.

In her past, Jenny had dated both women and unstable men, but during the course of our friendship it had been her habit to date pleasant, attractive younger guys. This would have been fine if she had been a casual person, or if a relationship hadn't been a high priority for her. But I knew that wasn't the case. I was thrilled for her when she met Adam, an average-looking, socially awkward man, someone her own age. *He's so old, so clumsy!* I said to myself. *Now* this *is the man for Jenny.* He seemed like relationship material, and Jenny loved his family, particularly his mother. Later, I would wonder if his mother was half the reason she stayed with him.

I took Adam's almost painful awkwardness as proof he was a good person. Instead he turned out to be manipulative and controlling. Soon she was coming to me with outrageous tales of him demanding she do things. In particular he wanted her to cease contact with a male friend. Jenny understood this to be an unreasonable request, and only chose to go along with it because the guy in question wasn't a close friend, and it was important to Adam. Humoring Adam wasn't good enough, though. He tried relentlessly to force a concession. He needed her to admit she had been wrong to be friends in the first place.

Another battle ensued when he insisted she needed to atone for all of her previous sexual partners. Considering that the two of them were unmarried and intimate, this was somewhat confusing. Ultimately, however, his insistence worked too well. He had never included himself in the list of people who had turned her into a harlot in need of salvation, but she converted to his religion, Catholicism, and decided to refrain from sex until marriage. To this day I feel smug relating this. She wasn't trying to prove a point; she had adopted his beliefs. I had been determined to convey to her that she shouldn't let him push her around, but instead let *me* push her around, so it felt hypocritical to put up much of a fight. Before long, it seemed to me she didn't have a single familiar personality trait left.

After Jenny began to change, but before the transformation was complete, she would often incredulously report to me on Adam's outrageous positions. "He told me my mom was going to hell because she's not Christian, and he said the guy at the quickie mart should learn to speak English!" Initially, these things would enrage her. Later she would explain to me that when she calmed down and thought rationally, she could see that he had been right all along. It became a regular occurrence.

Adam had broken my friend, and oh, how I hated him for it. For his part, he was aware that I saw him as a textbook emotional abuser (in her saner moments, Jenny agreed this was true, but didn't seem to see it as a call to action). This didn't endear me to him either.

Seeing him in this relationship made even his own mother nervous. In spite of, or more likely because of, how much she liked Jenny, she took the first opportunity to privately warn her. "He's my son and I love him, but he has always been this way. Of all my kids, he was the one who clung; I couldn't put him down for two full years. We had to kick him out because he was relentless. He made me feel like I was crazy. He won't stop." He had perfected his manipulation techniques long ago.

Adam's mother was right. And he had a way of taking everything as a personal insult, seeing the offer of any other point of view as a betrayal. Jenny's violent upbringing had predictably left her with an exaggerated startle reflex. This made him feel like she was afraid of *him*, specifically, which infuriated him. He took to sneaking up behind her when she was walking alone at night, then getting angry when she jumped.

"I used to feel," Jenny explained, "that if you're allergic to something, you should just avoid it. Adam believes that you should expose yourself to it and build up an immunity."

"It's not *his* allergy!" I raged. In fact, there was no allergy. No woman, and probably very few men, should deal with that kind of exposure. I wondered what Adam would prefer Jenny do when confronted by a strange man in a dark, deserted place. Give him a big kiss?

I'd made friends with a joyful, healthy person, and she was devolving before my eyes. I confronted her. "Do you realize that since you've been with Adam, you're sick and unhappy all the time?"

It was easier to observe these things from the outside, so I thought maybe she wasn't aware of how dramatic the change in her was, or how directly it could be traced back to the beginning of her relationship with Adam. I expected her to either deny it, or admit her relationship wasn't healthy. I hadn't counted on the possibility that she would agree, but not care.

"Yes. I'm different now. Take it or leave it," she told me firmly.

I had two weapons left in my arsenal, two things she still cared about—her love of bad action movies, and her sister's upcoming visit. I would try both. If they didn't work, it would be time to give up.

Jenny had always adored action movies, but rarely watched them anymore, and then only with a nagging guilt. Adam, who was pursuing a PhD in philosophy and believed he possessed a mind so superior he shouldn't have to do anything but think, had decreed that there were three morally permissible ways for a person to spend their free time—reading, writing, or drawing. Movies didn't fit.

"What about gardening? What about exercise? Or people who actually work instead of reading all day, and can't do anything with their free time but rest their bloody calluses?"

Jenny just sighed.

The truth was, my position on action movies was closer to Adam's than I cared to admit. I detested action films. It was, however, a bullet I was more than willing to take in order to prove I loved and accepted Jenny for who she was and Adam did not. I sat with her through an especially long and punishing blockbuster. She appreciated this, but couldn't enjoy it. When the movie was over she felt that we had not only wasted time, but had sinned.

Her sister would be visiting soon, and I knew she was wary of Jenny and Adam's relationship. I planned to invite Jenny's sister to dinner at my house when she visited. We would get Jenny alone and then what? Some sort of tag team? No matter, we would figure it out later. For the time being, all I needed was Jenny's ear and her sister's support.

The day Jenny called me and told me her sister had suffered a panic attack and had been unable to board the plane, I knew all hope was lost. It was time to give up.

Jenny had once told me about a former best friend she had adored, back when she was able to allow herself such an emotion. "Every love song on the radio was for her," she'd told me. I'd thought it was sweet, but now, as I drove around in my car at night singing along to Tracy Chapman's "Give Me One Reason" with my whole heart, it wasn't so sweet.

The Chapman song asked for one reason to turn around. One reason to stay. You can call me anytime, it entreats. I knew then that it wasn't going to happen.

I was sincerely heartbroken.

I didn't like the person she had become. I actively hated Adam. Jenny, who had once been a happy, free-spirited bisexual woman who worked at Planned Parenthood, was now very conservative. We disagreed on most things. During a conversation in which I refused to call Angelina Jolie a bad person because she was, to quote Jenny, a "home wrecker," she told me

I was "morally flexible." It was obvious she was talking about more than celebrity gossip. This seemed rich coming from someone who had flexibly flipped many of her moral positions over the course of time, but I couldn't be angry with her. There was hardly any of her left to be angry at.

Jenny still existed, but not as I'd known her. It was infuriating to see someone I cared about become someone else, especially when I thought so highly of the person she had been in the first place. Although Adam, a Catholic, hardly belonged to a fringe religion, his own blend of philosophy, morality, and religion made him seem less human to me. Like a soul belonging to a cult so unsuccessful it had attracted only one follower. And now Jenny. Perhaps this is typical—remove the flawed belief system, and the process remains the same. An abusive relationship doesn't seem so different from a cult. Both change people you love, threatening to usurp them altogether. Those of us standing on the sidelines are no match for either. We watch helplessly, scrambling for something to do, until we're ultimately forced to accept that we're powerless. The only hope is that the person you wish to save will, in her own time and her own way, save herself.

I have reason to be cautiously optimistic about the outcome of Jenny's relationship with Adam. Perhaps he wasn't as sure of himself as he'd seemed, because they put things on hold while Adam entered into intensive therapy. During this time they lived across the hall from each other, but didn't speak for months. Before social media was a normal part of daily life, they set up an elaborate system of communicating with no face-to-face contact. When they were confident Adam had sufficiently improved himself, they were married in a reverent Catholic ceremony. I wasn't invited, nor would I have expected to be.

I did not support the Jenny who had become a different person in order to please a man who didn't come close to deserving her. But perhaps the truth isn't so black and white. It could be that the Jenny I thought I knew had never really existed in the first place, that she was a shape-shifter, using the abused child's heightened perception to give whoever was in front of her what they needed. Maybe she gave me an impostor and became her authentic self with Adam. Or perhaps the real Jenny hasn't emerged yet. It could be that dozens of other Jennys have existed, each true in her own way, each former friend remembering her as whatever they wanted her to be.

About a year later, I saw her at a mutual friend's wedding. I was seven months pregnant with my second child, and she was eight weeks along with her first. Enough time had passed to allow us some thrill at seeing each other. We chatted happily the entire time. Even Adam and I were cordial. He took everything he did seriously, and looming fatherhood was no exception. He asked me about their work schedules, and whether one of them should stay home with the baby.

I advised him to do what was best for them. In my opinion, what the baby really needed were happy, relaxed parents, so they should do whatever would be most likely to produce that.

"But you stay home, so you must think it's the right thing to do," he pointed out, still unable to grasp that I didn't think like him, that what was best for me was not always best for everyone. But I could finally see there was nothing sinister in his motivation. He wanted to do the right thing, and he wanted my opinion on what the right thing was. He couldn't understand my moral flexibility.

The conversation contained many of the old elements that had once made me crazy. He paid rapt attention, just as he always had, and seemed to be looking as vigilantly as ever for inconsistencies he could use to invalidate everything else I'd said. It didn't enrage me anymore. Now I didn't see a narcissistic, abusive friend-stealer. He was just another struggling soul trying to make a connection. We all have good reasons for being who we are, and each one of us is desperately doing whatever we can in an attempt to get our needs met. Adam gets to do that too. Either that, or I'm just that eager to believe Jenny has a happy life, even if I can't be a part of it. He told me he was sure their baby was a girl.

Jenny and I had a great time at the wedding, and the two of us acknowledged that we wished we could be friends the way we had been before. But we both knew we couldn't, and made no attempt to pretend otherwise. When it was time to go, we said good-bye without exchanging contact information.

The last time I saw her was in a local boutique that sold free-trade gifts from around the world. I was buying a gift for the child of the same friend Jenny and I had seen married a few years earlier. I heard a familiar voice behind me.

"Erin!"

I turned around and saw Jenny. Her adorable son, now a toddler, slept in his stroller. I was filled with genuine affection. We embraced, and she filled me in on her life as it was now. Her job, her apartment, and Adam, who had scaled back on his doctoral work to stay home with their son. I toyed with the idea of ditching the baby shower and having coffee with her, but she didn't have the time anyway.

Early in our friendship, Jenny had told me she would never be able to have children. She said she couldn't stand the sound of a child crying. It didn't irritate her. It hurt her. She was thrown back into her own early pain—experiencing every public tantrum, expecting that every angry adult she might witness could cause genuine suffering. But I knew any children she might have would have a different childhood from her own, because *she* would be their mother. Jenny had been shocked at my suggestion that she would be able to give her own children something different from what she'd grown up with.

Was I right, or simply naive, believing someone could snap their fingers and break a cycle that had probably been going on for generations? Jenny's well-meaning mother had probably never planned for her four children to grow up in a war zone, but in spite of her best efforts, they had. When Jenny's son tells his own story, will it be that of an imperfect but basically happy childhood? Or will it be the story of a controlling, verbally abusive man who relentlessly chipped away at his wife until there wasn't a trace of the plucky, funny, and joyful girl she used to be? Will Jenny's son know that that girl was ever there, that she survived for more than thirty years before being flattened? We tell the women we care about not to bother—guys like that don't change. But I have to hope this is just a precaution, and what we really mean is, "I suppose there's an outside chance he might change, but finding out isn't worth the gamble."

I'm afraid to gamble. In my life there is no college roommate to call, no childhood best friend who knows me like a sister. No actual sister, either, although I suppose if my brother and husband are my most enduring contemporaries, I should be grateful. I am grateful. Deep down, though, it's not the same. I have a solid marriage, happy, healthy children, a career. But the close-knit group of women I think I should have, that we see in the media, just doesn't exist. Like a romantic who has been burned more times than she can count but still believes in true love, I keep trying.

I continue to struggle with why this is, not proud of the fact that I harbor guilt, anger, and sadness toward many of my ex-friends. Not Jenny, though. I did everything I could, and I know she did too. A painful breakup somehow produced the cleanest break. It gives me some peace to be able to wish her peace, along with joy and happiness, and if that means I have to wish the same for Adam, it's his as well.

Erin Eramia, LMHCA, is an individual therapist with a private practice. She is currently working on a novel, and blogs at openmindedskeptic.blogspot.com. She lives in Tacoma, Washington, with her husband and two children.

Part Five:
Making Sense of It

Finding meaning in the negative spaces.

Notes on Being Dumped: Aid for the Perplexed

Judith Podell

When you lose your lover
Miss that sweet jelly roll

When you lose your sister
Lose a piece of your soul

—"BFF Blues," Memphis Earlene Gray

The sudden death of my friendship with Luanne Tolliver at Hanging Rock Writers Colony twenty years ago remains a mystery and also a chronic source of pain and self-doubt. Nonetheless, with firm belief that it's better to carry a flashlight (even a crummy one) than to curse the darkness (no greater darkness than the human heart), I offer up these few notes and observations. Needless to say I have taken liberty with some of the facts and all of the names but not with the essential truth.

1. There's no protocol for rupture. You were *friends*, not lovers. "I want to be free to date other people" does not apply. Neither does "It's not you, it's me."

2. Sometimes you don't know why. Sometimes you do but it's too shameful to admit to. Sex with your BFF's ex shouldn't be a deal-breaker, you'd think, and you'd be wrong.

3. Dear Sister/BFF/Soul Mate: Please forgive me for (check the ones
   that apply):
   a. Sleeping with your lover, husband, family member, agent,
      shrink, Pilates instructor, contractor, or mechanic;
   b. Copying your hairstyle, outfits, or mannerisms, or displaying
      any other behavior reminiscent of Ingmar Bergman's *Persona*
      or creepy roommate movies starring Jennifer Jason Leigh; or
   c. Other, because I haven't a clue

4. You were *friends*, not sisters. Blood ties are much harder to break.
   Sisterhood is involuntary and you don't get to pick.

Luanne and I had different versions of the same idolized dead father.
Brilliant, mercurial men who'd been in World War II, both of them
thought *Catcher in the Rye* a waste of time and urged us to read *Catch-22*
instead. Luanne's father, a famous writer who died young of liver failure,
said *Catch-22* was the best novel to come out of World War II. My father,
an engineer with anger management issues, called it the most realistic. Not
just about World War II, he said. *Catch-22* was revealed truth, like the
second law of thermodynamics.

I had no idea what he was talking about, which is what happens when
you read Great Books before you've had Life Experience.

To be frank, I found *Catch-22* tedious, a guy's book with all the predict-
able irritations: cartoonish characters with cartoon names, lots of puns,
and no speaking parts for women aside from the occasional prostitute or
nurse. Joseph Heller took one joke and beat it to death: You'd have to be
crazy to want to fly combat missions. Pilots could be excused from flying
combat missions if they were diagnosed as too insane to fly a plane. Any
pilot could request a mental evaluation. Concern for one's own safety? That
was a sure sanity, under the applicable regulations. That was the Catch-22:
a self-perpetuating paradox from which there was no escape.

I've destroyed all of Luanne's letters, too painful to reread, especially the
last, where she accused me of banning her from the Hanging Rock dinner
table. A crazy accusation. How she got this idea remains a mystery. Was
she delusional or did she want to sever our connection so badly she'd lie? If
she believed me capable of such mean-girl malice, she'd never known me
after all. In Luanne's version the story of us would be a heartbreaking tale

of innocence, generosity, and trust rewarded with some inexplicable bit of two-faced behavior. In mine it remains Catch-22 for us girls.

5. Beware of girls who are writers. They'll encourage your secret and cherish you for the traits you feel obliged to curb in public.

Luanne's letters kept me connected to writing. She said my letters kept her sane. She lived in Tennessee, where she was surrounded by snake handlers, Republicans, and mendacity. Her only friend in town was the high school librarian, and he'd turned spiteful after she'd started getting published. I lived in Washington, DC, and worked for the IRS. "Kafka with a smiley face" was how I described my milieu.

We met at Heathcliff Forge, a writers' colony in Vermont. Our studios overlooked mountain pastures dotted with grazing Holsteins. I remember fresh air that smelled green—a poignant mix of hope and cow shit. It was late spring. We shared the same dank cinder-block kitchen and often got into conversations over coffee. I'd brought my French press coffeemaker and a pound of ground French roast from home, necessary fuel. Luanne drank only herbal tea.

We had different types of nervous systems, similar reading tastes, and reciprocal phobias. Luanne was afraid of spiders. I was afraid to walk in fields where there were cows. What if my presence provoked a stampede? Such huge animals, and surely they had right of way.

"Just keep walking; they'll get out of your way. They're *cows*," Luanne said, like this was self-explanatory, but she grew up in Alabama, not the New York metropolitan area, where, as I explained, we grow up thinking milk comes from a factory, the same as Coca-Cola.

Luanne's laugh was warm and welcoming. A mutual admiration society ensued.

At forty-two, I was one of the oldest writers, the only one without an MFA, and I felt like I'd fooled the border guards with a forged passport that wouldn't survive close inspection. Luanne's MFA came from the Iowa School of Famous Writers, and she'd won some prizes. Eudora Welty would have been proud to claim "Bruised Peaches" (*Prairie Schooner*, Honorable Mention) for her own. I told this to Luanne *before* I even found out that Eudora Welty was Luanne's own personal literary True North.

"Send it to the *New Yorker*. They're always looking for new writers,"

Luanne said, after reading my story that got rejected by *Ploughshares*, the *Paris Review*, and *Nimrod*.

Who knew the *New Yorker* never read its slush pile?

"That's the start of your novel," Luanne said of the fifteen-page letter I wrote her after my father died. In hindsight, perhaps more curse than blessing, since I'm still working on it, no end in sight. Oh, well. Kafka never finished *The Castle*, either, I remind myself, which is what Luanne might have said by way of encouragement if we'd still been friends.

We were tremendous intellectual snobs, Luanne and I. Oprah's Book Club? Oh, *please*. All that uplift when we really know there are no happy endings, only suffering followed by death. Jane Austen? Overrated. Jane Bowles is much better. Read her aloud and you'll just bust a gut laughing.

6. Beware of Southern girls. They're obliged to be charming, which can make them seem two-faced to the unwary. "Come back real soon" is not a legitimate invitation.

I think it was Luanne who told me that all Southern girls aspired to be Scarlett O'Hara and Melanie Wilkes. I persist in thinking of Luanne as a Melanie, although the modesty about her writing and diffidence about her career were strictly for public consumption. An elfin beauty with delicate bones and a wide mouth, she was highly photogenic. The trick of it, she explained, was being able to make your eyes smile.

She was also a wicked mimic.

Luanne's a famous writer now, or rather she's formerly famous, albeit widely respected. Her second novel, a dark multigenerational saga about incest and treachery, sold poorly, a damned shame since it was a much better book than her best-selling debut, which was about a plucky orphan girl from an impoverished rural background who pulled herself up by her own bootstraps to become a medical missionary in China. Oprah picked it for her book club.

7. Beware of girls with at least one alcoholic parent. The dearest, closest most delightful friend sometimes snaps, and you realize from the look on her face, or that tone of voice, that you've actually been at sufferance. A warning would have been nice.

I keep trying to reconstruct those two weeks in late September at Hanging Rock Writers Colony in Western North Carolina where Luanne's and my friendship died without me noticing. I can give you only scraps. The weather: that faint aroma of burning leaves in unseasonably warm air. Summer was overtired, a party that had gone on too long but the guests wouldn't leave. A soundtrack: Lots of Enya. "Orinoco Flow" over and over, music that I now associate with the sharp headache that swiftly follows a champagne high. We lived and worked in cottage studios, none of which was in sight of another. Dinner was when we all came together as a community, I remember Luanne missing dinner a few times. And I remember a growing sense of something off between us. The last time I saw Luanne was when I was packing up to leave Hanging Rock. By then I knew she was trying to avoid me. We met on the trail—she was carrying laundry—and it was painful to meet her eyes. The expression on her face was a mix of scorn, accusation, hurt, and pity. I do remember her wishing me luck with writing my novel and the suggestion that I might benefit from Prozac.

8. Imitation is the most sincere form of flattery, but copycat behavior is creepy. Beware of the Ambush Makeover even if your closet is stuffed full of What Not to Wear. Beware of girls who seek acolytes.

I'm thinking of Astrid, the vegetarian cook at Hanging Rock. Tall and willowy, with Pre-Raphaelite hair, dressed California gypsy style, mostly in white with lots of silver jewelry. Blazing blue eyes, like a Siberian husky. She had a certain cult-leader charisma. Claimed to have cooked for Mick Jagger and Jack Nicholson. I got on Astrid's bad side when I asked if there was anything for dinner that didn't have chopped vegetables in it. Everyone else seemed under her spell. Including Luanne.

9. Being dumped by your best girlfriend shouldn't hurt more than being dumped by your lover, you'd think, and you'd be wrong.

Lewis was the love of my life, or at least that's how it seemed at the time, and the months we were together felt like true romance. A journalist for one of the wire services who'd turned down the chance to cover the White House to be a police reporter, he looked like Dashiell Hammett. Very old-school kind of guy, believed reporters shouldn't own dinner jackets or use adjectives. Turned me on to West Coast jazz, road trips on two-lane blacktop, and the joy of sex in cheap motels, but after a year I could feel him pull away. I held on as long as I could, being short on pride and womanly wiles, but one day he said he wanted to be free to date other women.

Recovery took two years but left no scars. Painful early months. Real life switched from Technicolor to the cold blue-tinged video of those gloomy British detective series where the actors mumble. Every day a bad hair day. On the other hand I could confide in my friends, who all concluded that Lewis was fatally shallow and that I deserved better. My best guy friend even offered to speak to "Tony from Jersey," who for mere chump change would take a crowbar to Lewis's new Miata (not his real car; I've given him an upgrade). Tony from Jersey was a joke, but even now the thought of being able to exact that kind of revenge makes me smile.

No jokes like that about Luanne. I told no one. It seemed shameful.

I wish I could remember Luanne with detached affection and forgiveness, which is the way I remember Lewis. If he's forgotten me I don't much mind, because he never really knew me, any more than Narcissus knew Echo. It is, alas, my nature to be a flattering mirror, to forget my boring old self for a while, putting all that attention into my new lover. Figuring out who it is he'd like me to be, trying on that role for size if it sounds at all appealing. I'll read his favorite books to complete the mind meld. When it's over I clean house and crawl back into my skin again. Good-bye to the Gore-Tex outerwear. Adios to the Native American knickknacks and the collected works of Carlos Castaneda. No irrevocable losses.

10. Beware of girls who are writers. Sensitive, easy to offend, and ruthlessly selfish. Not to be trusted. Holders of grudges we turn into fiction. Unreliable narrators of our own lives even when we claim to be telling the truth.

I saved hard copies of the letters I wrote Luanne because they contain some of my best writing. I no longer have access to that writing voice. Youthful, exuberant, trusting, unguarded. The voice of a long-lost friend, the person I thought I was when I wrote to Luanne.

Judith Podell is a fiction writer, book critic, and lapsed lawyer. Her work has been included in numerous publications, including Mademoiselle, The Village Voice, *and* The New Guard literary review. *She is the author of* Blues for Beginners: Stories and Obsessions, *and writes about the everyday blues at www.memphisearlene.com. She has performed stand-up comedy in bars. One bar, really, but it was in Ireland. She received her MFA from Stonecoast and lives in Washington, DC.*

Bridezilla or Chill Bride?
Which One Are You?
Take This Quiz to Find Out!

Alexis Paige

W omen Should Evoke an Aura of Mystery. I learned this while reading my Mom's *Cosmopolitan* magazine at ten, during the summer of 1985. My younger brother and I sat on a beach on Lake Travis, outside Austin, Texas, with Mom and a group of her women friends, all in their early thirties. I had read about such groups, seemingly indestructible bands of women who in books were described with words like *gaiety* or *sisterhood*, but they and whatever organism it was that governed them seemed, from my pudgy prepubescence, distant and effortlessly cool— attributes I could never possess. And then there were the immutable, indecipherable codes. You Can Never Be Too Rich, Too Thin, or Too Tan! Guys Don't Make Passes at Girls Who Wear Glasses. Be Lusty, Not Clingy! What did it all mean? Which kind of girl would I be? Certainly, and with some effort, a lusty, hairless one, sans bowl cut, ten pounds thinner, and with a Ken-doll boyfriend. Willpower! Styling Tips! How to Tell if He's Interested. (1. Does he turn his body toward you when he's talking? 2. Does he say your name a lot as he's talking to you? 3. Has he ever called you *after* a date just to say he had a great time?) I studied *Cosmo* intently and puckered my lips into the reflection from Mom's boom box, which blared Huey Lewis and the News.

The women made a semicircle out of their clickable, foldable beach chairs woven with brightly colored vinyl tube straps. Then came a choreography of hair tossing, satiny thighs shimmying out of denim cutoffs, and bikini and tube tops emerging from tasseled T-shirts. A chorus of clicking and throaty laughter and squeaking Styrofoam cooler lids followed, as Mom and her girlfriends set up their encampment and tossed each other Tabs or Miller Lites. I went to the public toilet and practiced a head toss and horsey smile in a dirty mirror, but while Mom and her friends looked wild and graceful, I looked deformed, possibly even mentally retarded. My eyes were too close together, like my dad's, and they seemed buried in my face, like cookie eyes peering out from blobs of dough, or like buttons sewn too deeply into their fat cushions. I also couldn't get my shoulders right, I had only fatty lumps where breasts should be, and my teeth were more David Letterman than Christie Brinkley. Sucking in my gut and closing my lips around my mouth, I huffed back to the beach and placed our towel strategically in Mom's long shadow, so I could read and eat Doritos in peace.

I had been carrying around the *Cosmo* for days, at first like precious contraband and then openly, later, once Mom had noticed it and nodded her approval. It turned out there were a lot of things that women should do, most of them a rough calculus for male attention, female jealousy (or sometimes admiration), and losing weight and learning how to smile properly. Why Some Women Attract Men Like Crazy. What to Do with Your Mouth that Will Drive Him Wild. So far the only thing I knew how to do reliably with my mouth was shoot water like a spigot from the gap in my front teeth or stuff chewed-up food (bread worked best) under my upper lip and then smile and dumbly ask, "Excuse me, sir, is there something in my teeth?" I had read the magazine twice all the way through, taking mental crib notes about bikini lines and suntan oil and how to be "confident, never intimidating." (Stand up straight with your shoulders back and breasts at attention, make steady eye contact, but don't forget to smile. Confident posture can seem less severe with a practiced smile.) I had practiced Christie Brinkley's abdominal routine every night in my room before bed, but I still slouched or stood with my double-jointed knees bent backward into a grotesque crescent shape. I had spent hours that I can never get back glowering at myself in the mirror.

I was determined to be a different creature by the beginning of seventh grade that fall, when I would attend the much larger junior high where gorgeous gazelles roamed freely and trampled trolls like me. It was Josh's and my first summer with Mom since my parents' split a few years earlier. Going forward, our new life would be set in New Hampshire with Dad most of the year and now in Texas with Mom for school vacations and summers. One of the things I liked about being at Mom's was access to the mysterious intoxicant of femininity. Though Dad insisted that mine was the Dorothy Hamill, my brother and I got the same bowl haircut at Supercuts, we ate pizza and Burger King, and aesthetics were mostly ignored by my father, a man who wore corduroy suits and military-issue stapled eyeglasses. But Mom filled her life and her house with beautiful things: high heels, scarves, girlfriends, perfume, manicures, trendy clothes, lipstick, magazines, flowers, and crystal bowls of potpourri. My best friend and her sisters had one another for mascara tutorials and outfit checks, but I just had Dad, a five-year-old mimic, and bad cowlicks.

"What's *vindictive* mean?" I asked Mom, tapping her on a slender, freckled shoulder. She lifted up sunglasses from the bridge of her nose and eyed me with amusement. A breeze from the lake stirred her soft auburn hair, and spidery rivulets of black streamed from her eyes. She wore a tube top and red nail polish, and her long, slim legs seemed to stretch out a mile in front of her.

"What are you reading, honey?" she asked. I held up the magazine.

"Let me see that," she said, and looked at the article I was reading, "Can You Trust Your Girlfriend With Your Man?" Mom held up the magazine and swiveled around to show it to her friends. The women tossed their heads back and laughed, and Mom said, "Not if he's rich or attractive." A conversation ensued about girls' girls and the other kind, the "vindictive" kind. I took furious mental notes. (1. Does she seem more interested in seeing you when you're with him? 2. Does she seem more primped when your man is around, or does she flirt just a bit too much? 3. Does she seem guilty?)

Everything I came to believe in my formative years about women, female friendships in particular, was a mash-up of these *Cosmopolitan* platitudes, the toxic shit my mom and her friends said and did to one another, the toxic shit my friends and I mimicked, and other assorted myths that I observed in gym class or read about in Sweet Valley High. So I was utterly unprepared for what real female friendships looked and felt like and for how to behave once in them.

When I developed my first girlfriend crush a few years after that summer in Austin, I was still pantomiming bad *Cosmo* feminine mystery. But there were moments of freedom, lovely interstices when the codes fell away and I could just be myself—silly, smart, passionate about the environment, excitable in the classroom. The summer I was thirteen and entering high school in the fall, I shared a cabin with the Beatles, sweet woodsy Rebekah, and other female campers on Black Pond in rural New Hampshire. I don't remember the other girls' faces, only their bathing suits, splattered like neon spitballs all over the rough-hewn wood floors and wadded up in the window casements, collecting a fine powder of yellow pollen. And I remember that the cabin smelled like the wood shavings of a hamster cage and that every night Bekah and I and the amorphous others would count my mosquito bites—everyone piled onto my bunk, with Bekah aiming a flashlight at my legs, which were dotted with fresh pink welts among the older scabs. My legs were ugly—hideous, even—but I didn't care; I was as happy as I had ever been that summer, in that cabin, with those girls.

We were at Conservation Camp, an educational camp, where we engaged in outdoor activities while studying the environment. We took water samples and tested their pH in the same pond where we swam and canoed. We made thick sheets of paper from a gluey, all-natural pulp and wrote messy letters home on them; we hiked up to Franconia Falls, stuffing ferns into the brims of our hats to ward off mosquitoes and seas of black flies. We studied the area's impressive flora and fauna, a display of biodiversity that included spectacular creatures with chewy names I loved reciting: diving beetles, bladderwort, bogmat, frogs, mink, crayfish, sundew, turtles, mergansers, ospreys, and my favorite, the great blue heron. Whenever a heron alighted from the soft ripples it made on the water's surface, I imagined that the bird carried your wish off with it to be born. At night, campers and counselors gathered in the mess hall and sang folk classics like "If I Had a Hammer" and "Imagine" while swaying together in a citronella glow.

Rebekah was the first girl I met who validated my nerdiness and whose self-confidence about her own suggested that there was another way of being in the world that didn't include tasseled Whitesnake T-shirts, Aqua Net helmets, or the coarse, aggressive language of the Boston suburbs. She was starting at Kimball Union Academy in the fall, a fancy prep school for the super wealthy or the super smart, while I would return to public school—that uncouth dump where boys copied off my papers but never asked me out, and where the towering Ora Lemere stole my gym shorts and lied about it to my face, even as she wore, with obvious difficulty and possibly superglue, said gym shorts. I remember because they were red with a white stripe down the side, and as I confronted her on the sidelines of the basketball court, I wore borrowed shorts from Coach that were rolled over twice at the waistband and cinched with a belt improvised from a shoelace. I wasn't a confronter, except when a principle was involved, and so I mustered my courage, stood shakily on that principle, and asked Ora Lemere if she had accidentally put on the wrong gym shorts because hers looked a lot like the ones that, um, seemed to be missing from my locker.

"These are mine," she said. Then, "Wow, I didn't know you could talk. I thought you were like, whatchamacallit, like those people that can't talk."

"Like a mute?" I offered, helpfully.

"Yeah, that! Good one, Ex-Lax!" she said, slapping me high five. It was an unfortunate nickname I had picked up in elementary school when a couple of jerks thought Alexis was a weird name, one with a striking similarity to the brand-name laxative. "What a trip, Ex-Lax can talk!" Ora exclaimed loud enough for the whole class to hear. And then she ran around the gymnasium, high-fiving everyone, while I adjusted my borrowed shorts and walked toward the bleachers.

Unlike me, Rebekah seemed to know a secret about herself and the world that no one else knew: what other people thought of her wasn't particularly important or interesting. Her favorite band was the Beatles, and after I went home, I thought I could possess Bekah's secret for my own if I just bought and listened to all the Beatles tapes I could find at our local Strawberry's Records. The girls I knew from junior high listened to Def Leppard and wore Great White concert T-shirts, frayed up to their navels. They smoked cigarettes in the bathroom while talking about mackin' on boys at the school dances. These were the girls who rocked in the arms of their boyfriends at those same dances, while I sat in the corner eating pizza and waiting for Stephanie or Amy or April to come crying to me when Aaron, Mike, or Sully started grabbing some other girl's acid-washed ass.

Rebekah was different. As we steered a canoe through a thicket of high reeds, she explained the cultural importance of *Sgt. Pepper*, how the *White Album* was a departure from their earlier work, and how John Lennon was the most talented, with George Harrison a close second. I enjoyed these excited lectures, but I liked it best when she sang: "Lucy in the Sky with Diamonds" or "Norwegian Wood" or "Michelle," even the French parts. I rowed better when she sang, falling into a rhythm with her melody, pumping my arms cleanly so as not to make loud splashes, and gliding across the mirrored glass of the pond. Rebekah looked back and smiled, then belted "Blackbird" in a lucid, soaring soprano. It was like she was singing a secret truth, about everything that was possible, for us, for her, and for me.

Conservation Camp was a place and time where I began to consider a larger world, not too much larger than my world at home, but just enough for me to see past junior high. With some imagination I might even see beyond the smallness that the codes and strictures conscribed. It was a cusp time when I was still the girl before the woman, when my friendships with other girls were still everything.

Every time after, I would choose boys over my girlfriends—whether it was making out with so-and-so's boyfriend, or leaving umpteen girls' nights on the back of a motorcycle or in a taxi, or losing friends to my wanderlust, alcoholism, or serial dating. When it came to female friendships where men were involved, I didn't know how to stay. I always went off with some guy. The Artful Pickup. The Bedside Manner of Bachelor Girls. Your Girlfriends Will Forgive You in the Morning! Are You a Loyal Friend? (1. You're out with your girlfriend at a bar, flirting with a cute guy, when suddenly your friend says she doesn't feel well and wants to go home. Do you A) Give her ten bucks for a cab and tell her you will call her in the morning? _Yes, duh!_, or B) Grab both of your handbags, head back to her place, and offer to run out for ginger ale? _No, I'm no Florence Nightingale.) After that summer on Black Pond, I shot up six inches, my body leaned out, and I became, if not popular, someone who suddenly had more male attention than she knew what to do with. I became insatiable, too, high on my new superpower, ultimately defenseless. My intelligence didn't matter; all of my early awkwardness, combined with the codes, had set me up for this toxic femininity. A woman was a man-eater, a barracuda, or, as my waitressing buddies teased me, a shark. My conditioning had caught up with me.

By my early thirties, I had codified a minimally revised system of bullshit beliefs that further encoded a false choice between men and women. Women Are Difficult. Drama Queens. Guys Are Simple. So when my fiancé and I moved from city life to rural Vermont seven years ago, it felt both like starting anew—away from the city where I had been to jail, sought alcohol treatment, and entered recovery—and like going home, returning even to innocence. Inevitably, however, I was also leaving behind an important group of friends, some whom I had met in treatment and one a former drinking buddy and bestie who'd supported me through early recovery and after.

Emily stayed with me through the chaos and self-absorbed pontificating of late alcoholism. She stayed as I became someone else, more sober (less fun), serious, tentative, and contrite. Emily was wild, funny, a stunning gypsy with black hair, blue eyes, and a deep, throaty laugh. I had been drawn to her immediately when we met at the wine bar where I bartended and she managed; she was magnetic, confident, warm, fiercely loyal, and occasionally explosive. Though not fickle like some women I had known, Emily could lash out (mostly at those who had wronged friends and family) with a volatility that pushed my conflict-avoidant buttons. I drew her fire only once that I can remember, when I first started dating Keith and she pointed out that I had been missing in action and that friendship required mutuality. Emily was right, of course, but she had struck the deep fear that I was a shitty friend, and instead of accepting her observation, I was the one to lash out.

In the embarrassing text war that ensued, I surprised myself with my own nastiness, my own volatility, and my own tendency to say "fuck it" and run at the sign of challenge. And here was the chink in our friendship, or in my own makeup, that would foreshadow my later response in a more serious rift: I had always suspected that I could sustain friendships only temporarily, only for as long as I could pull off the fraud that I was worthy. I didn't know how to do conflict with women, but after some cooling off and well-timed laughter, we worked through it. Ultimately, I respected Emily's ability to challenge me, and I admired her volubility: she was as free with her compliments as she was with her barbs, her hugs, or her truth. I became determined not to leave her behind.

By the time my fiancé and I began planning our rural Vermont wedding a couple of years after our move, Emily and I were still in constant contact—trading visits, cards, and calls. She had even offered to help me set up for the DIY event, and I was grateful because Emily planned gorgeous, creative events for a living. With her help, my wedding wouldn't sag from sad homemade tissue-paper flowers or lame favors. But as the wedding got closer, she still hadn't booked a plane ticket or made lodging arrangements, every corner of my apartment was stuffed with sad tissue-paper flowers, and I began to worry she wasn't coming. So when I got an e-mail from Emily just a couple of weeks before the wedding, asking about airports and accommodations and other logistics, all the information I had included (in painstaking detail) in the original invitations, I was pissed. If anyone could pull a last-minute rabbit out of a hat, it would've been Emily, but instead of her usual spontaneity, I heard carelessness. Rather than interpret the e-mail as an innocent request for information or as an overture for help setting her up with a crash pad in our landlord's empty apartment, I read it as Emily begging off, as her reneging on a promise to help with and come to the wedding. Fair or not, when she mentioned that money was tight, I heard that my wedding wasn't important enough to save for, to plan for. I heard that I wasn't as cool as the beautiful and seemingly indestructible crew she now ran with on exciting trips to Vegas and, if memory serves, South America.

I was hurt, but somehow I couldn't just say that. Instead, I wrote back that her questions would be better fielded by my brother, with whom she was close and who was not in the last-minute panic stages of planning a wedding. She responded immediately, calling me a bridezilla and saying, "Don't send me any more of your neatly penned bullshit." And here it was again, the toxic knowing I mistook for wisdom or intuition: that women would eventually hurt and disappoint me if I let them in, that women were not to be trusted. I had always waited for the inevitable vindictiveness, instability, or menace that I believed encoded our chromosomal identity. So I struck first, and in a moment of emotional whiplash and through stinging tears, I sent a reply. "Don't bother coming," I said. *Me? A bridezilla?* (Bridezilla or Chill Bride? 1. Your middle name is Jordan Almonds. 2. Your deepest wish is to have your wedding Instagram pics featured on *The Knot*. 3. The bouquet toss *will* feature a Beyonce-esque dance routine to "Single Ladies," and your single gals *will* participate, or else, they *will* be eliminated. 4. Input about anything from floral arrangements to seating charts is A) A casual, everything-will-evolve-as-it-should affair. _Sure, whatever, it will all work out_ , or B) 'Whatever' is not in my vocabulary: every detail, down to the lining of the fork tines, will be choreographed, and anyone who wants to be involved must have Maid-of-Honor-level security clearance.) *Me?* The girl with fifty guests and homemade decorations, whose venue rental amounted to two bucks per car? *Bridezilla?* How dare she!

Bridezilla became the reason, the scapegoat, and bridezilla ultimately became the story I told others about the dumping. But the truth was I didn't really care about the insult. It was absurd, maybe even funny, something I would've chuckled about with Emily herself under different circumstances. What hurt was that my wedding didn't seem a priority. What hurt was her calling my too-careful boundary setting "neatly penned bullshit," for in my still-fragile three years of sobriety, neatly penned was the only way I knew how to stick up for myself. I was still learning so much about how to simply be, in this body, in my own feelings, and in this world.

But I hadn't yet learned how to do conflict with women, so when Emily responded a few hours later to my "Don't bother coming" kiss-off that I was breaking her heart, I ignored it and relied on my most reptilian coping mechanism: flight. It was over; the barrel had gone over the falls. When my mom became difficult, I cut her off for months at a time. When things got weird with friends, I bottled it up or became consumed by a new romance. Sometimes I just moved. I didn't know how to stay through pain or peskiness. With girlfriends, I didn't know how to work through their or my own ugliness, how to fight for the friendship. So I left because it was easier, and the story went that she broke my heart. The story went that no one calls me a bridezilla and gets away with it. The story went that we had merely grown apart, had different interests. But the truth was I had broken my own heart with pride and stubbornness and timidity. And I fought for three years with this pride and stubbornness before I finally responded to Emily's last e-mail. *I was wrong. I miss you. I miss us.* I would have to learn how to fight for the women in my life. I would have to learn how to fight, ultimately, for myself.

If anything, this is as much a story about dumping as it is about love, fear, and hatred of women. You internalize misogyny, swallowing it hard and whole and driving it down into your bellies. You play its roles, perpetuate its cycles, and become alienated from other women, just as you are alienated from yourself. A system doesn't care about people, only about survival, only about itself.

Women are difficult, you learn; women are gossipy, small, vindictive, dramatic, competitive, backstabbing, vain, selfish, slutty, stupid, emotional, mean, shallow, materialistic, and without intrinsic value. Insistence makes the lies seem true; just ask Fox News. And after a while you believe what you've heard about women, and invariably about yourself, and one day some guy, a stranger, calls you a cunt in public for sticking up for someone else, or your boyfriend calls you a slut, or a dear friend calls you bridezilla, and eventually you can no longer separate yourself from the machine. You can no longer remember your own innocence.

Alexis Paige's work has appeared in Passages North, Fourth Genre, The Rumpus, Pithead Chapel, Ragazine, 14 Hills, *and others. Winner of the 2013 New Millennium Writings Nonfiction Award, she also received recent nominations for a Pushcart Prize and for the Sundress Best of the Net Anthology, as well as a "Freshly Pressed" feature on WordPress. Twice a top-ten finalist of* Glamour *magazine's essay contest, Paige holds an MA in poetry from San Francisco State University and an MFA in nonfiction from the Stonecoast creative writing program, where she served as Creative Nonfiction Editor of the* Stonecoast Review. *She is an assistant editor and blog contributor for* Brevity *magazine, and she lives in Vermont, where she is writing a memoir about the 60-day stint in a Texas jail that taught her how to grow up. You can find her at alexispaigewrites.com.*

Maybe After December

Heidi Griminger Blanke

Susan initiated the severance, cutting the ties of our friendship, if it was even a friendship. With three quick words, she completed it, slicing the last threads so deftly I was rooted speechless.

The world around me dropped away and I saw the scene as if from above. I stood alone, the disposable friend. If, as I have already said, I was even a friend at all. Though I couldn't have known it at the time, her words would haunt me for months to come, causing the occasional sleepless night or teary remembrance. Deep down, I recognized it was her, not me, who was the lesser friend, but a small part of me continued to question that conclusion.

That was two years ago, and even now I can barely summon the courage to be angry with her, though I should be. If I had worked harder at our friendship, would it have mattered? Or would circumstances have played themselves out in an *Alice in Wonderland* kind of way, my self-confidence growing smaller as I swallowed her words, while she seemed to grow taller as she spat them out?

Susan and I met at the small university where we both taught. Our offices were within shouting distance of each other, bookending the drinking fountain. We really didn't have much common ground, other than being colleagues. Susan taught courses involving calculations and graphs and I taught courses about people. She was ten years my junior, the single mother of two daughters. I'd been married, to the same man, for over twenty-five years, with the luxury of working part-time when my children were young. She was tall and I was short; she loved the country and I loved New York City. Yet we had in common a passion for our academic focus, a respect for our students and for each other, or so I thought, and the willingness to put up with the glass ceiling for which our religiously based school was known.

When Susan came on board, I'd already been teaching for five years, having assumed this second career as I settled into middle age. We both had the requisite book-filled offices, philodendrons, advisees, committees, and whiteboards for student notes glued to our office doors. Susan's office soon acquired an old club chair for student lounging and a floor lamp for ambience. I added an old kitchen chair I'd painted and reupholstered and a table lamp I'd refinished with crackle paint. Susan brewed tea in her office; I had a coffeepot. Nonetheless, we caught moments here and there to complain about administration and talk about how the women in our department dressed up so well, while those in other departments wore jeans, stodgy skirts, and dresses from the 1980s.

Susan and I didn't see each other outside of work, and some semesters we taught opposite hours and rarely saw each other at all. I dropped my youngest daughter at the bus stop each morning and came to work early, with plenty of time to brew coffee before stepping into the classroom. Susan exercised in the morning, dropped her daughters at school and day care, and then zoomed to work with barely enough time to unlock her office door before racing to her late-morning class. We couldn't have been more opposite, yet we connected in those subliminal ways of which women are capable, that sense of knowing what the other is feeling or needing without saying a word. We talked about our kids, our students, and our approach to teaching. Things that I found important and that I was sure she valued as deeply.

I missed the signs we were growing apart, never thinking our paths were diverging. Now I know Susan was the one going off trail, while I remained glued to the regular route. She no longer wanted to go for lunch, as she was training for her first triathlon and ate a prescribed diet that didn't include creamy soups and cheesy sandwiches. In contrast, I was baking up a storm, working my way through a new dessert cookbook. Susan started seeing a man, but never wanted to go out with my husband and me for a movie or dinner. Even our teaching methods suddenly emerged on either side of the Continental Divide, with Susan increasing the number of tests and quizzes she used and my giving them up completely for essays and group projects.

When I stopped by her office one day, coffee mug in hand, and plopped into her club chair, she made polite conversation for a few minutes, then told me she had piles of work to do and asked me to leave. I was hurt, but only slightly. After all, I reasoned, it was getting toward the end of the semester and Susan no doubt had plenty of grading to do.

I eventually quit my job, having had enough of the glass ceiling. Over the next few years, I sent Susan an occasional e-mail, but she never answered. I convinced myself they must have gone to spam.

Susan remained with the university a few more years before leaving as well. I was immersed in nonprofit administration and she opted for the corporate world. My new job was fulfilling, my husband and I became empty nesters, and I forgot about Susan.

Two years ago, I ran into her on the sidewalk outside an office complex. I was helping with a food drive, wearing shorts, a logo T-shirt, a baseball cap, and sunscreen. I'd gained another five menopausal pounds. Susan was on her way to work, her tan and toned legs emerging model-like from her short skirt, her hair dyed to look as if the sun knew exactly where to highlight it. I beamed hello and reached up to hug her. She retreated a nearly imperceptible step when I did.

We exchanged the usual pleasantries. Other people were within earshot, so there was no easy way out. I asked about her kids, her job. She answered dutifully, but briefly.

"We should get together for coffee sometime," Susan suggested.

I might have simply rejoiced at the invitation, but instead I was stunned. Susan wanted to resume our friendship. Finally, I answered. "I would *love* to. Here's my card," I said, placing it in her palm. "Let me know what you have free in the next couple of weeks."

I couldn't wait to catch up. I wanted to know about her job, if she was still racing, how her kids were doing, if she was still dating the same person or perhaps had even married.

"I'm really busy right now," she replied. "Maybe after December." She turned to go, a couple of employees catching up to her side as if they were groupies.

Those three words.

Maybe after December? It was August. We were no longer tied to a semester schedule. I swallowed my pride and my heart. Susan didn't want to have coffee with me. I don't think she cared if she ever saw me again. Let me rephrase that, I *know* she didn't.

Even now, I replay the scene over in my mind more often than I should.

I wonder where I went wrong, or if I was the one who went wrong. Did I do or say something to alienate her, or did she move on, simply no longer requiring whatever my friendship originally had to offer?

Did I have nothing to offer?

Maybe after December. I've skated past two Decembers, balancing those three words on ice riddled with these new cracks, doing my best to keep her words from dumping me into the frigid depths below the surface of my confidence. Hadn't I done just fine until she showed up again? I'm doing my best to navigate my way back to solid ground on my own road, as I have been, just fine. Without the slivers I had once accepted as friendship.

That day, Susan unknowingly taught me a lesson. I learned how important it is to be a presence in a friend's life, to make time, all the time, not just after December.

Heidi Griminger Blanke, PhD. is a freelance writer in La Crosse, Wisconsin. She has published in Threads *magazine and* The Wedding Magazine *(La Crosse, Green Bay, and Rochester), and writes regularly for* La Crosse Magazine, Coulee Region Women *magazine, and other local publications. Her essay, "The Bunion Kicker," was featured on the Erma Bombeck Writers Workshop website. Two of her articles, "The Path to a Beach House" and "A Family Lives Here," were part of a 2013 Minnesota Magazine and Publishing Association Silver Award to Coulee Region Women in the category Regular Column. She is a member of La Crosse Women Writers and leads the Express-oh writing group. Prior to her writing career, Blanke was employed in nonprofit administration and academia.*

Out of the Blue

Mary Ann Noe

Her name was Veronica.

Okay, her name wasn't Veronica. It's a stupid pseudonym, now that I see it written. Let's call her Kelly instead. Which isn't her real name either. You can make up one for yourself, if you want.

This is a tale of friendship, nothing more, nothing less. No love-hate, no same-sex relationship, no broken marriage. Simple friendship. That turned out not so simple.

Considering how close Kelly and I were, you'd think we'd known each other forever, or at least since high school. But she appeared ten years into my teaching career. That's misleading too, because I took a nine-year break in there somewhere, so I was really closer to forty than thirty years old.

Anyway, one a.m., Blank-Blank Oregon College, Ponderosa dorm—was that really its name? Doesn't matter. I'd been asleep for, oh, about two hours, after trying to stay awake to meet a roommate who was a complete stranger. Thirty of us had been chosen to share a month of studying Shakespeare under the auspices of a very nice monetary grant. Turns out the Powers That Choose made sure we came from every corner of the nation, small schools and big schools, urban and suburban, private and public. Very inclusive. I was from Wisconsin. Kelly was from . . . well, let's protect anonymity here . . . somewhere out East.

By post-suppertime, Kelly was the only one in absentia. My designated roommate, late. That didn't bode well in the greater scheme of things. When she wasn't in by midnight, I gave up waiting and drifted away to Dreamless Land.

Until one a.m., when the door banged open and a loud whisper apologized for launching me about four feet straight up. "Kelly's plane was late," a coordinator's voice floated in.

I was having none of it. "Welcomeseeyouinthemorning," I mumbled, dismissing them both with a weak wave of my hand. The door closed and a few minutes of thuds and rustles finally subsided into silence.

Sigh.

The next morning proved prophetic. At least for the good stuff. We both awoke at exactly the same time.

I opened one eye and discovered a matching one across the narrow room, albeit blue instead of hazel, prying itself open. We both smiled. At least as well as we could with our faces crammed into the pillows. She slept on her stomach too.

"I'm Kelly," she said, mostly into the pillow.

"I'm Mary Ann. How come you're up so early?" The low slant of light gave away the breaking dawn. I raised my head enough to see the clock. Five a.m. Nothing new for me.

"I run," she said.

At that point, I sat up. This was going to be a marriage made in heaven. "No one else is up." The hall was absolutely silent. "I run in the morning too. Well," I hedged, "I really only jog. But I love this time of day."

By then, she was sitting on the edge of her bed. The room was so narrow we almost touched knees. Typical dorm room. She smiled. "Well, let's go, then." She jumped up, T-shirt barely covering her pink panties, and reached for a pair of running shorts.

I shifted to make room for her and slid out of bed. T-shirt and beige panties. My running shorts even complemented hers. This was an auspicious start.

"Which direction?" she asked, as we both continued dressing.

I pointed out the window toward the rolling Cascade Mountains across the valley. "That's not the way to go. I explored last night and there's a highway in the way." I swung my arm to the right. "Head south for California. They say it's only thirty miles away."

She exploded into laughter. "I run, but not *that* far."

"Me neither. Outward bound twenty minutes, then I'll turn around. Maybe I can beat the traffic to the shower that way."

She nodded. "That should put me right behind you when I come in."

"We can tag-team, then." I grinned and raised an eyebrow. "This is a coed floor, so we have to share the communal bathroom."

That brought another burst of laughter. "Shower, too?"

"No, thank God."

By that time, we actually looked like runners. Sports bras, T-shirts, cushy socks, proper footwear. We locked up behind us and slipped down the stairs, careful not to wake anyone deliberately.

In spite of the hour, a hearty voice greeted us. "Mornin', ladies." Ed, from Florida, coffee cup in hand. "Early birds too, I see." He frowned. "Out to sweat, are you?" Ed was chunky, like a fire hydrant. Definitely not hard-core exercise material.

Without even a glance at Kelly, I pretty much knew what she was thinking. *Keep moving!*

"Coffee'll be waiting for you when you get back," he said as we opened the front door.

"I'm more a tea person," Kelly called over her shoulder.

My thoughts exactly.

"Duly noted." Ed's voice faded behind us.

Our timing was impeccable. She arrived back at the dorm just as I was emerging from the shower. Others were up, but she got my spot. The hand-off was perfect. The rhythm of mornings persisted throughout the month, never varying by more than a few minutes. Ed even added tea to his morning coffee ritual.

Over a very few days, she knew I was married with two kids, sang in the church choir, and loved to travel. I knew she was divorced, had no kids, and shared an upper flat in an old Victorian with another woman. The accountant who lived downstairs owned the place and did her taxes, but was not of romantic interest. I knew she worked a second job in a very classy restaurant, in an old stagecoach inn, where she wasn't allowed to write down customers' orders. She knew I'd sold sewing machines before teaching high school. We both worked with freshmen and seniors and had similar classroom styles. We both loved music of all kinds.

That became important later.

On our first free Saturday, we joined a group heading out to tackle white-water rafting. When we reached the river, the guide came around to hand out life vests and assign us to one of two big inflatable boats. Kelly and I recoiled at the same time as he came within a nose of us. When he moved on, Kelly leaned in and whispered, "He smells like a sweathouse! Maybe he'll fall overboard and improve the aroma." We stifled laughs.

Once on the water, we repented our curse on the poor guide. The river, fed by snowmelt from the mountains, was frigid. A dunking would have been unpleasant, to say the least.

After a half hour of vigorous paddling, our guide pulled up to the bank, warning us of rapids and a sure drenching around the next curve. "Anybody not comfortable with getting really wet and bounced around a lot should get out here." He bumped against a flat boulder and held us steady while handing passengers out onto dry land. "Just follow the path and you'll come out down below, where we'll pick you up. It follows the river, so you'll have plenty of opportunities to take pictures and heckle the poor souls in the boats." He turned to us, two of the four who remained aboard. "What about you guys? Sure you don't want to walk around all this?" He flung out a gesture toward the noisy rapids.

"What?" Kelly hollered, then laughed. The roar of the water barely left enough room in our ears to hear his questions. She gave me one of those looks that said, *Is he kidding? Of course we're ready!* Simultaneously, we gave him a thumbs-up.

By the time we pulled in to pick up the ninnies who'd chickened out on the rapids run, Kelly and I, soaked to the bone and hysterical with laughter, were stuck to each other for good. We sloshed out of the boat and dumped out our shoes. "Didja get our picture? Didja?" we asked in tandem. Once assured that our idiocy had been recorded for posterity, we gave everyone else big hugs, ensuring that no one would go home dry.

Every day, when the group headed into the town center, Mary Ann and Kelly walked the mile and a half, while most others took the shuttle. When restaurant menus were perused, Mary Ann and Kelly invariably ordered the same things. When urgent shopping excursions called out, Mary Ann and Kelly were automatically included. When hikes in the mountains were proposed, Mary Ann and Kelly bent to lace up their boots. Drink after a play? Sure, we both said. Cheesecake at the tiny bakery? We squeezed in and ordered the vanilla-strawberry-blueberry. Did we like that Shakespeare poster? We each bought one. Cliché or not, we became the Siamese Twins.

Someone proposed a weekend trip to the coast and we jumped on that bandwagon.

Kelly: "If we go we're gonna have to—"

Mary Ann: "Rent a car. To save time we should—"

Kelly: "Pack food for the road. Do you know if—"

Mary Ann: "Yeah, Lynn rented a condo for the bunch. It's all arranged."

You get the idea.

We packed two cars and set off south to see the redwoods, and then headed west to the ocean. For two days, we meandered as far north as we could get before swinging back to the rubber band of interstate that would eventually sling us back to our starting point. No one else arose early enough, but Kelly and I checked for low tide and crawled around rocks and tidal pools, searching for—I had no idea what for. What did I know? I'm from an inland state without tides or seals or starfish. We discovered purple starfish—who would've guessed? And strange-looking barnacles waving little fingers, as if searching for a handhold somewhere. But the best was watching a seal play a game of catch with a salmon. Well, the salmon probably wasn't too happy, as it was the one being tossed into the air and caught by a seal doing a back float. Finally, even the seal—or was it a sea lion?—grew tired of those antics. It embraced the fish and bit off its head. Salmon for breakfast. Granted, it wasn't smoked and there were no bagels, but still.

A photo from that trip says it all. We stand, each with one arm across the other's shoulder, outside arms akimbo on cocked hips, cameras dangling from our wrists. Both of us in jeans and hiking boots. Both of us in T-shirts, with sweatshirts tied over our shoulders and binoculars hanging from our necks. Both of us in sunglasses and baseball caps. Both of us smiling.

That may have been the beginning of the end. Then again, maybe not.

I think probably not. Instead, it was probably the apex. Kind of like the top of the curve of a plot line, where everything's supposed to go downhill from there. Or the point in the movie where all is fine, but you know someone is about to pop out of the closet with a bloody knife. Of course *you* know it'll go downhill. *You* know something wicked is about to happen. But the characters don't. I know we didn't. We most certainly did not. Not yet, anyway.

Once we got back into our usual routine, we began to spend our personal grant money. Time was running out, after all. We'd be home in another week. All of us began to stock up on teaching aids for our classrooms, our planning, and our students. We bought guides and plays, Shakespeare and costume coloring books to create bulletin boards. We bought everything we could to bolster our insider information—who knew that sci-fi writer Isaac Asimov wrote a fat book on Shakespeare's plays? A really good book too. Kelly and I instituted a regular routine of visiting the bookstores and the festival store after every play, just in case we'd missed something.

That's when we hit on our Grand Scheme. We both loved Renaissance music, especially the live performances given in the square before every play. The singers had recordings. The recorder quartets had recordings. Plenty of luscious music to choose from. These were the days of cassette tapes and vinyl records. Even with money from our grant, they didn't come cheap.

Thus the scheme: Kelly would buy some. I'd buy some. We didn't have access to recording equipment where we were. But we did back home. It was supremely logical to share. Once back home, we could use our resources and copy to trade. Might I add, worries about music piracy wasn't really publicized back then and didn't even cross our minds. We were more focused on our tight budgets.

This, right then, right there, was likely the beginning of the end. Though, once again, we appeared blithely unaware. Well, at least I was blithely unaware. I can't say whether Kelly was blithely aware or not.

The rest of the week gave no indication of anything different. We woke, we ran, we ate breakfast, we saw plays, we discussed and studied, we stayed up late and talked. Then, we packed. With the first van readied for the airport, we hugged each other. We hugged everybody, all thirty of us in a big hugfest.

I'm stalling.

Kelly left before I did, so I helped her tote and stow her luggage. We didn't know what to say to each other, so we hugged. Then we cried. I can't believe it: we both cried and promised to send off our copied tapes as soon as we could. She was going to Florida for a week, so I built that into my mental calendar.

Then she was gone, waving out the window, along with everybody else in the van, until we couldn't see even the taillights anymore.

I made it home without problems. I unpacked. I hugged my husband and kids. I did laundry. I made copies of the music and sent them off. I had my pictures developed and grinned at the memories. I waited until I knew Kelly was back home from Florida and then I called her to make sure she'd received everything. Her roommate answered. "She's not back from Florida yet. She'll be back later. I'll tell her you called." Total length of conversation under twenty seconds.

Okay. She'll get back to me. Or her music will show up in a few days. All right, fine, more like a few weeks.

Two months later? No call, no package. I called and left a message. No response.

I'd make one more call. In fact, I'd wait another month until her birthday. That's a good reason to call, right? Her roommate answered again. "Sorry. Not here right now. Bye." Wait, wait! I explained the whole share-and-share-alike thing and got, "Okay, I'll tell her."

I waited. Weeks. Months. My last effort was to send a Christmas card and ask if she got the music and had she sent mine out yet? No response. I threw in the towel.

What happened? What in hell happened? Had Kelly truly just forgotten? Was she in a relationship with her roommate and figured a friendship with me would get in the way? I never talked to her on the phone, so maybe her roommate was a woman consumed with unfounded jealousy and never passed on my messages. Maybe she even intercepted the mail. My speculations traveled further and further afield. None of them made any sense to me.

I'd never been dumped with such finality. Actually, I'd never been dumped before. Okay, by boyfriends, but that was to be expected. Yes, friends had drifted away, but we were both aware of the shift. This time, it came out of the blue.

I thought I'd get over it. It still surfaces on some mornings when the air is just so and I sling a sweatshirt around my shoulders. When I'm sitting in the dark watching yet another production of *A Midsummer Night's Dream*. When someone tries to finish my sentence and doesn't get it right. Those memories bring up sepia-toned images, nothing more. But when I come across that photo of the two of us, I'm still blindsided.

I wonder what I did. Or maybe what I didn't do? I know one thing: I'll never figure it out. And I realize I don't have to.

Mary Ann Noe has been writing since she could first pick up a pencil. After teaching literature and writing she retired and began to practice what she preached for thirty years, publishing short stories, nonfiction, and poetry, and photography. Her short stories have appeared in Quality Women's Fiction, Haruah: Breath of Heaven, *and* Main Street Rag. *Her non-fiction, "Wisconsin's Glacial Drumlin Trial" and "The Thuringer Forest in Germany" appear in the online travel magazine GoNOMAD.com, and poems have been published in Bellowing Ark and Essential Inklings.*

Simple Geometry: The Art of War for Girls

Nina Gaby

1 *A polygon can have any number of sides.*
There is something profound about failure. It's humbling, of course, teaching us to get up nine times after falling ten, or is it the other way around? It allows us to weep knowingly at Beckett quotes on refrigerator magnets. We can look back on it with a sense of nobility for our survival. Phoenix rising from the ashes. Maybe that's pretty hokey, but sometimes hokey is just the comfort you need.

Why am I even telling you this? Because I failed miserably in front of an audience not of my choosing and it has taken me years to place it within a tolerable framework? And how did that audience become one *not of my choosing*? I still don't know. Failing with friends around to help you get back up is one thing, this was quite another.

"Nothing bad can happen to a writer. Everything is material," is a quote attributed to both Garrison Keillor and Philip Roth, depending on which icon is in one's best interest to channel at any given time. I have believed in the concept since my first diary entry at age seven, accumulating piles of notebooks to prove it. Piles of scribbles looking for structure, for answers, and now for a formula to explain how a set of seemingly hopeful choices, a kind of gosh-darn-it, leap-and-the-net-will-appear-just-do-it-ism went so wrong. I look for an equation: if I had done this, would that have happened? What if, what if? Don't we all do this? Look to make sense of our failures? I sort through the fifty years of notebooks on paper and the ones in my head.

More recently, and in my own estimation a perfect balance of Keillor's droll optimism and Roth's bitter irony, the scribbling perseverates on how I dragged my family from a perfectly good life to one of marginalized chaos. All of it based on the idea that we would have a better life (envision polygon sides one, two, and three). What follows is the story of how I came to believe that could happen: a better life, my search for connection, and the shit that we do to one another under the heading of friendship.

As a kid I learned the deliciousness of gossip. My family was built on triangulation (the bad kind, the kind that family therapists decry). But isn't the triangle the most stable geometric form? I could never understand why it was considered such a bad thing. If you liked Grandma Yetta, you couldn't like her sister Tante Celia. If you favored my sister, you couldn't like my cousin. Choose my mother, you couldn't like the other daughter-in-law. Long, intense discussion ensued, often one-sided and in Yiddish, as I overheard my grandmother on the phone with my mother, with her cousins. Whoever would listen. In my family you were in or you were out. Right corner, wrong corner. Made sense to me.

Perhaps like me and my friends, you engaged in that macabre pastime, that magical thinking, of imagining your parents dead. I imposed a variation of this rule onto my little sister: we couldn't play this simple childhood game of what we would do if *both* our parents, for example, got killed in a car crash or something equally dramatic. Our rule was that *one* parent *had* to survive. Either Mom, who was okay when she was sober, or Dad, who was okay when he was drunk. We had to choose just one. In or out. The ensuing guilt, in its childish way, was lively and excruciating. I started to look for this rush everywhere.

We had a neighbor, Marie. Why I think of her is this: she never had a good thing to say about anyone but me, and I easily resonated with the tone that set. With her, I was always in.

As kids we roamed the neighborhood. We'd eventually end up at Marie's, at the end of the street where her backyard faced the rest of the neighborhood, congregating briefly. Then the others, especially the boys, would move on, but since Marie told me I was "special" and that she really liked talking to me because I was smarter than the other kids, I'd throw down my hula hoop or my bike and we'd settle in the lawn chairs for a good gossip. Who knows what a seven-year-old has to gossip about except people in the neighborhood, like my parents, whose resounding drunken arguments were no secret, but there we'd sit until my mother yelled across the street, calling me home on some pretense. She hated Marie, always wanting to know what we were talking about. I went from triangle to triangle. Someone was always out. And if memory serves me, it was always a woman.

Geometrically, things stabilized in fourth grade. I made new friends and found a square: me, Nancy, Carol, and Christine. Nancy and Carol were tightly bonded, best friends since kindergarten, living across from each other in a traditional 1950s neighborhood of sidewalks shaded by the few Dutch elms that had escaped the blight of the previous decade. I lived on the next street, and Christine lived way down the block in a modern house. Her father was a professor; they were recent Eastern European immigrants. Her ethnicity only became important years later, in junior high, when Christine tried to steal my boyfriend and I, probably fueled by some Ronettes song and too much nicotine, slapped her in the hall by our lockers. Her father presented himself at our house that night. He told my father that a slap in his country was an invitation to a duel to the death. My shocked father asked if grounding might be an adequate punishment. More than adequate: For the next two weeks I could watch Christine and my two-timing Danny get off the bus together from my window. They both dumped me.

But way before that happened, the square—Nancy, Carol, Christine, and me—provided a template for an ever-changing diagram of alliances. Diagrams based on tidbits of knowledge, observations of our world that offered a prepubescent power almost sexual in its capacity to enfold us. We drew lines between and against each other. Carol and Nina against Christine and Nancy, and when another piece of knowledge emerged, another dyad would huddle on another set of front steps, gathering energy against the other two, somehow making it safe to talk about the world, about our crazy new bodies, our parents' shortcomings, whatever came into our heads. Talking talking talking. Passionate triangles formed by the splitting of the square. *The Art of War* for girls.

And then, like an Etch A Sketch, the lines drawn, connections found, with a shake it all disappears.

2. *Projective planes and the one-point perspective line*
To what degree would a diagram help define the pain of losing one's grip? Could some sort of algebraic topology, a set of truths, make it better? God knows we don't have any rituals to mark the passing of friendship. No guidelines for when projection trumps perspective. No Adele song for us when it all goes south.

Nancy and Carol faded long before that fatal slap by the lockers, not yet interested in boys or cigarettes or any of the things I was now into. I think Christine ended up in a private school soon after she dumped me, a place far away from our neighborhood where high school could lead to better things. Her parents weren't any happier about their daughter dating Danny than mine were, nor did they ever get over my act of delinquency. But before that I'd easily found another best friend. No one was important for very long.

I was a gregarious kid, full of the anxieties I know now are part of childhood for many, but I was bright and funny and very capable of making friends. I never would have dreamed that I wouldn't. My parents were a popular couple; the importance of a social circle was ingrained early on. Picky, I easily rejected people who didn't meet a certain standard, that standard reflecting whatever I was most interested in at the time. Bike riding, playing Peter Pan, later on gossiping about who was wearing a bra, and then on to boys, cigarettes, alcohol. I tended to change best friends like brands of cigarettes or favorite pop songs, with the ease of a gigolo. Until Linda. We were thirteen, had purchased the *Meet the Beatles!* album together. We went steady with boys who were best friends, Danny and Wally. We all wore black. We were a pack.

Danny and I broke up a lot, even before Christine, over silly things, like if he didn't call or meet me on time, or send me a note, or sign a slam book. Linda followed my lead and made life as difficult for Wally. Then we would listen to our British groups and girl groups and the likes of Dusty Springfield who "only wants to be with you," over and over and over, together, on the little portable phonographs we had in our bedrooms. The breakup agony was somewhat delicious, shared with my best friend like a fluffy pastel mohair sweater. Safe, insular, invincible. If they'd had those little split-heart charms back in 1963, we would have each worn a half.

By fall we had made the change to high school. Linda and I met up at the corner store every morning to ride the bus together. One morning, school was off for teacher conferences, and I assumed we'd hang out at Linda's because both her parents worked and we could smoke all day. I had moved beyond Danny by this point, and outside of the slap and the grounding, I don't remember the end of that relationship in any of the detail that I remember the phone call that came during breakfast the morning of the conference. Linda's little sister was on the phone, hysterical.

"Linda's not your best friend anymore!"

What?

"She broke up with you!"

I put down my orange juice and tried to comfort Linda's little sister, who had obviously found stability in the linear certitude of the friendship. Maybe something she was aspiring to— the coolness, the safety. Her voice was shaking. "I don't want you to break up!"

Apparently another friend had stayed overnight at their house and I was the last to know. At that age it had the impact of an affair. "Sleeping over" was not a sexual act, but certainly the equivalent: someone else's teased-up hair resting on the pillow in what I felt was my second home was comparable betrayal. Linda's sister was crying. My little sister, open-mouthed across the breakfast table, also started to cry. My blood went cold, but I wasn't going to cry. I wasn't going to do anything. There was nothing to do. No ceremony, no songs for the phonograph. Even if I had acknowledged the depth of loss, it would have been too weird to bear, like I was gay or something, which back then in our neighborhood was unthinkable. I moved on. Linda and I never made eye contact again. I kept the Beatles album. I still have it, somewhere in the barn along with the old 45s.

The breakup was more complicated than just that; it bore the complications of relationships we deem more important. My parents didn't particularly like Linda; she came from a blue-collar household and was in a lower scholastic track. We were Jewish living in a Catholic, working-class neighborhood, that being what we could afford, and it was where I felt comfortable. But my parents' affiliations were with the upper-middle-class Jewish professionals in their circle. Neither Linda nor Danny was acceptable. My parents wanted me to be friends with people who simply did not exist in our neighborhood. "Why don't you go out with Jewish boys? Why don't you have Jewish friends? These people you go with, they're never going to go to college. You're ruining your life!"

Early friendships were fraught with hypocrisy, contextual shame, and cultural marginalization, equations far too intricate for a thirteen-year-old. Dumping was a more complicated phenomenon than we ever acknowledged, and easier to do than to try to understand. I had to pretend it didn't matter. I learned to project a safer perspective onto a wall between me and the pain. It made me independent with a never-quite-fulfilled craving for closeness. Maybe that was part of the problem. The resultant sheer avoidance never made it any easier, not at thirteen, not at fifty.

Over time, a series of broken friendships ensued, as they do for many of us. Some were mutually agreed upon, or due to geographical attrition. Some had to do with hockey sticks (senior year in high school) or drunken gossip (for which I will always be sorry). I dumped; I was dumped. In a women's therapy group during the feminist era of the late seventies, I was able to ritualize one breakup by screaming and beating pillows with a plastic bat. "I want my friend back!" I shrieked, and was then embraced by a group of nonjudgmental women who were only too happy to help me acknowledge the pain. One friend dumped me when she got married. One friend dumped me when I got married. One group of feminist radicals dumped me for my vintage stilettos. One group of colleagues had to dump me in order to remain affiliated with another colleague who had more power in the system. Friends dumped me for being too drunk. Friends dumped me for being too sober. Sometimes the process is subtle, reduced to Twitter feed and the occasional electronic holiday newsletter.

3. *It's not the shape of the objects but how they fit together.*
When I was fifty, dissatisfied, burned out, and looking for an answer to my future, I got a surprise letter from an old friend. A bright and talented woman, and I will describe her in broad strokes, a composite really – a friend from more exciting times, of my long-ago life when I was free and traveled and was an artist. Nothing like my life at fifty—family fragmented, no social circle like the one that defined my parents' life at my age.

"Brigadoon" was how she described her community in that letter. Poorly versed in classic musical theater myself, I could not have known how apt the Etch A Sketch metaphor would become, how quickly connections disappear. During a visit to this old friend in her new and what I considered perfect life, I saw an entry point, the change I was looking for. I saw our circle—"community," as folks like to call it. I convinced my husband to leave our secure but uninspired life in Upstate New York. I took my little daughter out of a good school and tore her away from the grandmother she loved. We moved to the small New England village where my friend lived, bought a tired old inn on a dirt road, and settled in for what I thought would be the rest of my life in a ready-made neighborhood full of like-minded folks who really seemed to like us. I already had a best friend, how perfect. A friend who took great care listing with precision which folks were "acceptable" and which were not. But I ignored that, infatuated with everything. There were pretend regattas on the tiny lake; there were weekly board games with B.U.S.T., the village United Scrabble Team, in our dining room, complete with T-shirts. Everyone borrowed stuff from everyone. There was only dial-up Internet, minimal TV reception, and almost no cell coverage. We were always outside, like kids in a Rockwell painting, walking, swimming, snowshoeing. No one had house keys. Boundaries were permeable, or so it seemed, and life was fluid. I liked everyone. For a while, anyway, it was my New American Dream. My own *Newhart* show.

And of course, any entry point on a surface leads to a tiny crack, to fissures, to fragmentation. Complexities. So many people, all spinning around with their own significant problems and loyalties. It's easy to become the scapegoat for all that. When the cohesion failed, I was flung, dumped. I was out. I still try to understand: Which one of my new friends represented Linda; which one was Grandma? Marie? Christine? Who did I represent to them? I hadn't slapped anyone, didn't drink anymore. I had tried to not even gossip. But centrifugal force won and I was out.

The failure was that we failed. Within two months of our move, 9/11 happened. My friend and I were out walking in that beautiful September morning that no one will ever forget. As we got back to the village, skipping and dancing and singing Motown, her husband called her in to watch the TV. At first I thought he was angry that we were having so much fun. He told her what was happening; the second tower was just about to fall. I felt I was encroaching on an intimate moment between them, but I had no TV, so I stayed. And watched as America lost its balance, tipped on its side.

A few weeks later my husband and I closed the deal on the inn. We had been leasing it, I was running it, the summer had gone fine, and occupancy was more than adequate. No one could have anticipated what would happen to our hospitality economy, and beyond that, in the bigger picture, we Americans still had no idea that we were being swindled out of so much. The events of 9/11 became a huge excuse. But how was I to know any of this that September when we went right ahead and signed on the dotted line?

Soon business began to evaporate, as did our savings. We could barely get an insurance policy in this changing landscape, let alone renovate the inn and groom the cross-country ski trails and provide free coffee to the neighborhood in the morning and free wine and homemade snacks in the afternoon. People were pitted against one another in the dwindling economy. My husband returned to his previous career as a social worker. I did my best alone with the inn, but we had no resources to bring it up to the standard we and others had envisioned for the neighborhood. In my independent way, I probably rejected help even if it was offered, although my memory is not to be trusted on that.

And anyway, it was a small village with an ancient topology. This one seemed to hate that one and then that one hated the other one and then they all seemed to hate me.

4. *"In little towns, lives roll along so close to one another; loves and hates beat about, their wings almost touching."* —Willa Cather, *Lucy Gayheart*
In the beginning I found a great degree of comfort in looking out over the dark village late at night, small squares of light in the bedrooms of the other women who were up with their menopausal insomnia, their anxieties, their financial and relationship problems. A backdrop of connectedness despite the fragmentation that lay beneath the surface. Sometimes I would go across the road at midnight to float on my back in the lake, watch the stars, the windows, safe, held in the warm abeyance of the water. It almost made it worth it. And yes, there were kind and welcoming people around, but they paled in contrast to those who dumped us, to my friend who dumped me. It's all in the projection and the perspective.

I have my notebooks filled with the things that happened. Now I title them, Keillor-like, in my head like just so many funny little chapters: "The Yom Kippur Wood-Stealing Incident." "The Easter Yapping-Terrier Throwdown." "The Wedding Stealers." "The Mysterious Disappearance of B.U.S.T."

When the invitation for the annual "regatta"—neighbors on inflatable floating devices, in costumes and bathing suits, silliness followed by drinks and potluck—never arrived that second year, another neighbor similarly forgotten and I made a separate picnic for our kids, kind of an *alfresco salon de refusés*. The next summer, when one couple put an electric motor on their detachable dock, set it up with a table and chairs and nice linen, and carted almost everyone around the lake for floating feasts, we were among the few not invited. We could watch the floating dinner parties from the bridge, illuminated by candlelight on the dark lake. A scene from a foreign film we weren't part of. I wanted to see them capsize.

One stone tossed after another, or maybe just so many pebbles, my objectivity now suspect. "Freeze-Out at the Post Office." "We Want the Right Kind of People on That Committee." "That Blizzard When a Neighbor Wouldn't Let Two of the Kids into Her House" (my ten-year-old being one of them). I knew it was over the Christmas we didn't get any Puppy Chow. Puppy Chow was a tradition in the village, a surprisingly tasty blend of cereal and cocoa that looked like dog food, brightly wrapped in bows and cellophane and distributed to those on the right list. My husband was relieved. My daughter and I were devastated.

I can't go into more detail. It stops being funny real fast. You will quickly see me as pathetic, an unsympathetic narrator. A medieval shunning might have been only a bit more painful. But at least we might have understood how we'd broken the rules. For a while I believed that whatever I had done could be undone. But I didn't know what that was. These were kind people becoming so unkind. That doesn't just happen, does it?, you might ask. I don't know; I don't get the math. I failed in not knowing how to put two and two together. I guess we just weren't good enough. Or they weren't kind enough. Simple geometry.

I spent much of our third winter fat from Paxil. I lay on the couch for days at a time, unshowered, in a frayed bathrobe. I didn't move from the moment my daughter got on the school bus at 7:23 in the morning to the moment she arrived home, a down comforter over my eyes to shut out the light in the odd event of any sun peering through the gray northern New England sky. I was able to afford this luxury because I had nothing else to do. We were losing the inn to the economic realities of that time. I would jump off the couch at 2:43 when the bus dropped her back off, pick the stray flecks of down out of the corners of my mouth, and pretend that I had not just spent another day crazy. Our village was not populated by people I would have chosen as witnesses to my biggest failures.

My friends dumped me, like I imagine high school might have been for others; it just wasn't worth hanging out with the suddenly unpopular girl. The girl who couldn't even groom her ski trails. Who was, truth be told, pretty lousy at Scrabble. There were few phone calls when my mother died, when my dog died, my cat, my uncle, my cousin. When I had to sell the inn. Many of these women, bright and talented and with whom I had once, at least briefly, been friends, did not stand by me. A few did, of course, but I had expected, and needed, more. You know how men are; they hang back and look clueless. But with women there is always something else going on. I was just out. I should have just understood that.

You ask, how can I stay here? I stay here to write and float on the lake in the summer and stroll its frozen tundra in the winter. I stay here to keep the still-loyal friends back in my old hometown emotionally closer, so afraid that true proximity will ruin us. I'm also afraid, maybe superstitious, that this bad luck will follow me. So I installed a handsome lock on the front door, a symbolic gesture, perhaps. I got a good job, sold off part of the property. My family, more immune to rejection, likes it here.

The failure is not in what is; it is in what we expected it to be. I think I wanted to be like a small self-governing nation amidst friendly neighboring tribes, the landscape a study in continuity and connectedness. Instead, a black-and-white image sticks in my mind. A photograph in a gallery, or was it one that I took myself, wandering through the snow? The photograph is of a line of four upright fence posts, four stark black lines across a pure white field. Nothing else but the gradations of white. Who knew white had so many planes, so many colors? At first I was stunned by the crisp melancholy balanced by pristine hope. Now all I see are four lines. Nothing touching.

Nina Gaby is the editor of this collection and a writer, visual artist, and psychiatric nurse practitioner. Her fiction, nonfiction, articles, and prose poems have been published in a number of anthologies and periodicals, and her art can be found in a variety of collections, including the Renwick Gallery of the Smithsonian. This is her first book.

Sources

1   Aristotle thinkexist.com/quotation/friendship_is_a_single_
     soul_dwelling_in_two/220963.html

2   Anaïs Nin, *The Diary of Anaïs Nin, Vol. 1: 1931–1934.*

3   David Spiegel, quote authenticated via personal e-mail, July 21,
     2014.

4, 5 Vivian Gornick, *The Situation and the Story* (New York: Farrar,
     Straus and Giroux, 2001), 46.

5.   Ibid., 163.

6.   Marla Paul, *The Friendship Crisis: Finding, Making, and Keeping
     Friends When You're Not a Kid Anymore,* (Emmaus, PA: Rodale
     Books, 2004).

Acknowledgments

Creating an anthology is like creating a community. I am so very grateful to all the gifted writers who submitted their work to this collection, who so honestly, and with such grace, humor, and hard-won answers, joined me in exploring the often frail and unfathomable nature of friendship.

To Brooke Warner and Caitlyn Levin of She Writes Press and to Julie Powers Schoerke and Marissa DeCuir Curnutte of JKSCommunications. My team.

To Victoria Zackheim, Sharon Stiller, Fran London, Alexis Paige, and the guy at Kripalu who taught me the literary magic of geometry. Your very generous professional and practical support is so greatly appreciated.

To Sandra Warburton Barry, Alan Jefferys and Char Cutforth, hope there's a well-appointed library in heaven or wherever you are. Wish you could have stuck around long enough to see this become a reality.

To a bunch of people, in no particular order, who have just "been there," either reading, listening, sticking around, expressing opinions, arguing, being kind, or just making me laugh: Zoe Gaby-Smith, Josh Turk, Lauri Allenbach, Katherine Denison, Anne Seyffert, Martha Leonard, Linda Whalen Quinlan, Eva Weiss, Ben Powell, Sari Gaby, Lily Greiten, Rosa Spivakovsky-Gonzales, Eileen Peck Foster, Marjorie Barkin Searle, Fran Glover, Mary Sojurner, my fabulous Facebook community (you know who you are), Annette Welch, Chuck and Suzanne Montante, Barbara Hurd, Amy Ferris, Suzanne Strempek Shea, River Jordan, Al and Jackie, Sandy and Nancy, Mindy, Skip, Ted, and the Rowley clan—Jim, Shannon, and Kris.

To my loyal assistant, Chester, who sacrificed many hours of Kong play to help me with this endeavor. No one can feel dumped for very long with a golden retriever at her side.

To those who didn't even realize they were helping: Dinty Moore, Lee Gutkind, Bob Guccione Jr., Neil White, Jill Marsal, Yona Zeldis McDonough, Ed K., and the old postmaster who told me every day to stay safe out there.

And finally, to those women of my village, without whom this book would never even have been conceived. Thanks for dumping me. And a bigger thanks to those who didn't.

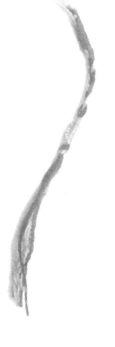

About the Editor

Nina Gaby is a writer, visual artist and psychiatric nurse practitioner whose essays can be found in collections by Creative Non Fiction, The Best of the Burlington Writer's Workshop, Seal Press, Wising-Up Press, and several periodicals. Her fiction has been published in Lilith Magazine, the Prose-Poem Project, and in short-story collections by Paper Journey Press. She works, writes and lives with her family in New England.

SELECTED TITLES FROM SHE WRITES PRESS

She Writes Press is an independent publishing company
founded to serve women writers everywhere.
Visit us at www.shewritespress.com.

Three Minus One: Parents' Stories of Love & Loss edited by Sean Hanish and
Brooke Warner
$17.95, 978-1-938314-80-3
A collection of stories and artwork by parents who have suffered child loss
that offers insight into this unique and devastating experience.

*Her Name Is Kaur: Sikh American Women Write About Love, Courage, and
Faith* edited by Meeta Kaur
$17.95, 978-1-938314-70-4
An eye-opening, multifaceted collection of essays by Sikh American
women exploring the concept of love in the context of the modern landscape and influences that shape their lives.

Seeing Red: A Woman's Quest for Truth, Power, and the Sacred by Lone Morch
$16.95, 978-1-938314-12-4
One woman's journey over inner and outer mountains—a quest that takes
her to the holy Mt. Kailas in Tibet, through a seven-year marriage, and
into the arms of the fierce goddess Kali, where she discovers her powerful,
feminine self.

Fixing for Love: A Memoir of Love Addiction by Shary Hauer
$16.95, 978-1-63152-982-5
An intimate and illuminating account of corporate executive—and secret
love addict—Shary Hauer's migration from destructive to healthy love.

Fire Season: A Memoir by Hollye Dexter
$16.95, 978-1-63152-974-0
After she loses everything in a fire, Hollye Dexter's life spirals downward
and she begins to unravel—but when she finds herself at the brink of losing
her husband, she is forced to dig within herself for the strength to keep her
family together.

*Flip-Flops After Fifty: And Other Thoughts on Aging I Remembered to Write
Down* by Cindy Eastman
$16.95, 978-1-938314-68-1
A collection of frank and funny essays about turning fifty—and all the
emotional ups and downs that come with it.

CPSIA information can be obtained at www.ICGtesting.com
Printed in the USA
BVOW05s0634290415

397700BV00001B/1/P